START YOUR ONLINE COURSE BUSINESS TODAY

DR HESHAM MASHHOUR

Start Your Online Course Business Today
by Hesham Mashhour

Published by Better Brain Lab
Office Number B-05,
Atom Building, Urban Walk,
New Cairo, Cairo
Egypt 11835

https://www.betterbrainlab.com/

Copyright © 2022 Hesham Mashhour
All rights reserved. No portion of this book may be reproduced in any form without permission from the publisher, except as permitted by U.S. copyright law.
For permissions contact: hesham@betterbrainlab.com

TABLE OF CONTENTS

Part I Opportunity

Chapter One *Determine Your Business Model & Set Your Personal Goals*
Chapter Two *Know What Level Of Course You're Creating & For Who*

Part II Potential

Chapter Three *Choose A Course Topic That Ticks All The Right Boxes*
Chapter Four *Develop A Course Outline From Your Course Topic*

Part III The Grind

Chapter Five *How To Create Engaging Material For Your Online Course*
Chapter Six *How To Price Your Online Course To Maximise Revenue*
Chapter Seven *How To Promote Your Course Organically*

Part IV Growth

Chapter Eight *Grow Your Audience & Online Community*
Chapter Nine *Diversity Your Revenue Model & Passive Income Streams*

1 Comprehensive
has everything you need to know

2 Exercises & Templates
to help plan out your strategy

3 Beautifully Designed
fully illustrated and easy to read

4 Insider Experience
from an author who launched courses with many clients

WHY CHOOSE THIS BOOK?

1
OPPORTUNITY

PART I

CHAPTER ONE

"DETERMINE YOUR BUSINESS MODEL & SET YOUR PERSONAL GOALS"

"If you don't know where you are going, you will probably end up somewhere else."
– Lawrence J. Peter

You're planning to create your first online course. No doubt you're super excited about it, as you should be! You're looking forward to creating a product from the ground up, sharing your knowledge and skills with your audience, and earning their respect — all while also making a living.

No wonder you're excited. I'm excited for you too.

However...

Creating an online course is an incredibly long and taxing process and I wouldn't be surprised if, by the end of your journey, you tell your friends and family that you've "birthed" an online course.

Several course creators I've worked with over the last few years have certainly felt that way. With so much going on, it's understandable that so many great educators end up feeling overwhelmed and lose sight of the broader picture. That's why I'm writing this book.

But first, let's take a step back and ask ourselves:

"What is it that I'm actually trying to do here?"

Because let's be honest, very few people will go through the trouble (and expense) of creating an entire online course just for the sake of it. Don't get me wrong, I love creating e-learning products. It's enjoyable and deeply rewarding. However, I can think of about a hundred other things that are also enjoyable and rewarding that aren't nearly as difficult or stressful as creating an online course.

So, why do we still do it then? **Opportunity.**

Starting an online course business in 2022 is one of the best decisions you can make. But don't just take my word for it.

I'll let you be the judge.

1. High Demand
Udemy has over 12 million students and only 20,000 instructors on the platform. That's 600 students each.

2. Growing Demand
The size of the global e-learning market grew from $165B in 2015 to $275B in 2022. The market size is estimated to reach $325B by 2025.

3. Increasing Acceptance
77% of corporations in the United States used some form of online education in 2017. By 2020, 98% of corporations offered online education programmes to employees.

4. Global Reach
While 70% of the e-learning industry is located in the United States and Europe, demand in Asia is growing at a whopping 17.3% annually.

I want you to know that creating an online course and building an online course business are two very different things. If what you want to do is to build an online course business, you must realise that the first online course you make is not your end goal.

It's simply a means to an end.

The end goal?

To build a thriving business.

Unfortunately, many educators don't make that realisation until they're much further along their course creation journey. However, knowing this crucial bit of information right from the start will give you a clear advantage and edge. You will base all your decisions on what's best for the health of your business and brand, not the course you're creating right now. **In other words, you'll go from having a short-term outlook to adopting long-term vision.**

Because your building what is essentially a lifelong business venture, you must first figure out what your personal life goals and aspirations are. What do you want most out of life?

"What does your ideal life and self look like?"

Your ideal self represents your most authentic self because it's who you want to be and what you want your ideal life to look like.

Figuring out who your ideal self is will allow you to determine your wants and desires, which will help you decide what business model works best for you and how you can incorporate your first online course (and all future course) into that ecosystem.

Your first online course should not be a standalone product, if what you want to do is build a successful business that you and your family can live off. Sadly, standalone courses are rarely all that lucrative.

That's why you must build a business and brand around your courses.

> ## *Online Course Case Study*
>
> One of my regular clients is a clinical hypnotherapist.
>
> She first approached me because she wanted to create an online course that would help daughters of toxic mothers overcome their trauma. Why did she want to create this course?
>
> Because in her ideal life, she saw herself helping hundreds (if not thousands) of women overcome their trauma. She didn't want to be constrained by geographic distance and hoped to help people irrespective of where they lived. The online course she planned to create worked in tandem with her hypnotherapy practice as part of a single and streamlined ecosystem.
>
> In other words, the online course wasn't a distraction but contributed to her business model and brand value.
>
> Moreover, she knew that once she launched the course, she would be able to sell it for many years to come, generating passive income, allowing her to become financially independent. With increased financial independence, she could take on more altruistic projects to help those in need but without the resources to seek help.

I can't speak for anyone but myself, so I'll tell you what motivates me in the hope that it resonates with you too. I hope that one day I become financially independent, so I can be in a position that allows me to take on whatever projects that I'm passionate about.

The only way to achieve financial independence is to create products that are able to generate passive income long into the foreseeable future. As an educator, you have the unique opportunity to create an online course, upload this course onto a membership site like

Skillshare, and see it sell for many years to come!

"Passive income" isn't about making you rich, and it's not about allowing you to retire early, though it can certainly do both these things if you want it to. At its core, passive income is about breaking the bond between your time and income so that you no longer have to spend your time to earn an income. Your livelihood.

Creating an online course can help you break that bond, so you can focus on the things in life that fulfil you. For me, fulfilment means the luxury to spend a nonsensical amount of time creating this book and labouring over its fine details. For my client, fulfilment is the ability to take on altruistic projects she stood to gain nothing from.

"What does fulfilment mean to you?"

Here are some ideas to get you thinking:
1. *Fulfilment* can mean having the time to challenge yourself
2. *Fulfilment* can mean the ability to contribute to others
3. *Fulfilment* can be the luxury of living in the present moment
4. *Fulfilment* allows you to connect with something larger
5. *Fulfilment* is freeing yourself from hypotheticals

Exercise #1

This is your first exercise in this book. Briefly answer the following questions to determine what your priorities are in life and begin uncovering your ideal self.

Q1. What traits do you admire most in the people around you?
-
-
-

Q2. What are the things that scare and worry you the most?
-
-
-

Q3. What does it mean to you to be successful in life?
-
-
-

Passive income and financial independence aside, creating an online course can help you in several other ways. It can help you:

- **Serve your customers better if you have an existing business.** Your online course can serve as an additional service you offer your customers. It can help you connect better with clients, as interacting with your course's audience will make you more attune with the issues that your customers face.
- **Launch a growing mailing list of keen customers.** You can use this mailing list to spark conversations among your community and generate ideas and promote and sell your products and services, including any online courses you make in the future.
- **Expand your reach and decrease your costs.** Why spend money on expensive marketing campaigns when you are your own influencer and can promote your products organically?

Moreover, remember that every piece of content you create for your online course can be recycled and reused in new and original ways. For example, once you complete your course, you can choose a few videos that work as standalone content and post these videos on YouTube, Facebook, or Instagram.

These standalone videos can be used to promote your course, grow your online following, and generate *even more* passive income.

Additionally, any print material you create for your course (a course guide or workbook, for example) can be reused to create blog posts, email newsletters, or can even be sold as a whole through Amazon's Kindle Direct Publishing (KDP) program. If you do decide to sell your book on Amazon, you can include links inside the e-book version that direct the reader to your website and course landing page, so they can purchase your course and subscribe to your mailing list. In short, it's a win-win situation for you and your business.

Crucially, you will also be able to leverage your content and influence to make a difference. You can do this by working with brands and other creators to raise awareness for issues you care about. You can empower those who are less fortunate by taking part in outreach efforts and creating scholarship programs for your students.

The bottom line is that your online course is content.

You are the creator of that content.

You own it. You can do whatever you like with it.

Becoming a content creator in 2022 is one of the best decisions you can make because it gives you enormous agency and offers a world of endless opportunities ripe for the taking.

So, will you be taking on this challenge?

If the answer is yes, you better fasten your seatbelt.

PART I

CHAPTER TWO

"KNOW WHAT LEVEL OF COURSE YOU'RE CREATING & FOR WHO"

"A goal without a plan is just a wish."
– Antoine de Saint-Exupéry

Before we discuss the three levels of online courses, it's important to understand why people go out of their way to buy our online courses when they can get the same knowledge for free online. Let's not kid ourselves...

As content creators looking to educate people and make money while we do so, we must accept that everything we have to teach our students probably already exists online — for free. In fact, it probably even exists in the same format (video) that you intend to use to create your online course. *YouTube, anyone?*

"If so, why do people still buy online courses?"

The most obvious answer is that your students are looking for a product with all the right information all in one place, so they can get the results they're looking for efficiently without having to spend hours scouring the internet. While that's certainly true, allow me to tell you a short story about me when I was sixteen years old.

A Walk Down Memory Lane...

As a child, I was fairly inquisitive. I guess I still am.

At the age of around sixteen, I got into the habit of illegally downloading dozens of online courses on just about every topic; everything from computer programming to video editing and public speaking. Because it was 2010 and we didn't have the best bandwidth at home, I'd go to my mother's office on my days off from school and download the courses while I was there.

It was the golden age of online piracy.

Surely, it must have been worth it? I must have learnt so much from all these online courses. *It's the reason why I'm so clever, no?*

No.

I actually didn't watch a single one of those courses, despite having worked so hard to find and (illegally) acquire them.

Why was that? I'm by no means lazy. I graduated from medical school and studied at the University of Cambridge. I spend my days seeing patients and invest my nights creating content. In between all that, I'm constantly learning new things.

So, why did sixteen-year-old me, who had infinitely more energy than I do now, not watch a single one of these courses?

I had no reason to.

Frankly, I had no one to keep me accountable and did not have the support an instructor provides, which is what sets a paid online course apart from the knowledge that's available online for free.

> ### Top Tip Time
>
> If you want your online course to be a success, it must include all the knowledge your students need to achieve the results they're looking for.
>
> Knowledge alone is not enough, however. To make a difference in your students' lives, you must provide them with accountability and support.
>
> Be an educator, but also be a coach.

The degree of accountability and support you offer your students will dictate what level of online course you create. It will also determine what type of customer you target with that online course. Generally speaking, there are three types of customers:

- **Interested Customers** are the people who only want your knowledge, which they hope to gain for free. These customers will be the ones to attend your free webinars and watch your YouTube videos. They'll sign up for your mailing list, hoping to access more free content every now and then. Sometimes, however, they're happy to spend a little money on your content.

Typically, courses for interested customers sell for $10-$50.

- **Qualified Customers** are invested in gaining results. They've probably already watched many YouTube videos and gone through a lot of free material. Now they're looking to level up and are willing to pay you a premium for a step-by-step system and your support and guidance along the way. Qualified customers want you to hold their hands, give them advice and feedback, and help them achieve their desired results.

Courses created for qualified customers often sell for anywhere between $250 to $1,000, depending on the support and accountability.

- **Committed Customers** are people in the market for a one-to-one customised program. They want your full support and dedication and are willing to pay you good money for it. When you work with these clients, you often become as emotionally invested in their journey as they are. You're their coach and mentor, but you're also their professional partner.

These courses will start at no less than $5,000 and have no ceiling.

THREE TYPES OF CUSTOMERS

INTERESTED CUSTOMERS

JUST YOUR KNOWLEDGE = $25-100

QUALIFIED CUSTOMERS

STEP-BY-STEP SYSTEM TO FOLLOW = $250-1,000

COMMITTED CUSTOMERS

CUSTOMISED PROGRAMME = >$5,000

CHOOSING THE RIGHT LEVEL OF COURSE TO MAKE

Now that you're familiar with the three types of customers and the different courses we make for each, you can decide what level of online course you want to make. Before you make that decision, however, you should think carefully about whether or not you're able to offer the level of support that a qualified or committed customer needs.

I recommend you set the foundations for your online course business by **targeting interested customers first** and developing your business model from there. There are three main reasons we do this:

1. Interested customers are much easier to find than qualified or committed customers. After all, there are many more people who are willing to spend $25-100 on an online course than there are people willing to invest $500 or more.
2. Interested customers are easier to draw into your community as you can offer them access to free content (a short PDF guide or pamphlet, for example) in exchange for their email addresses.
3. As a group, interested customers will provide you with a broad customer base that you can nurture and, over time, grow into qualified and committed customers. After all, all qualified customers were, at some point, interested customers.

And now, for the most important reason:

Selling a $500 course to your qualified customers will be orders of magnitude easier if you already have a community of interested customers to whom you sold a $50 course. *Why?*

Because you will have already established yourself as a credible educator. Your community will already know the quality and value of your work and will, therefore, be significantly less apprehensive about spending $500 on a more advanced course.

It will be much easier and much less expensive to promote and launch each new course you create. You'll already have a community of users who will grow with you and continue to take each successive (and more advanced) course you make, as you go deeper and deeper into your niche of choice.

In short, your first course or e-learning product must appeal to the largest number of people interested in your niche. Once you've captured those people's attention and established your credibility, you narrow down your focus to create "offshoot" courses about more advanced topics within the same niche.

All the courses you create must belong to the same niche.

If you start creating random courses that don't belong to the same niche, you won't be able to effectively promote them to your community. You will need to start your content and market research from scratch. You will need to identify and approach your target customers from scratch. You will need to build a relationship with these people (who have no clue who you are) — from scratch.

It would be as if you were creating your first online course again.

That's so much work. Why are you making your life so hard?

Why... when you already have a community of interested customers who've already purchased one of your courses and, based on that behaviour, will likely consider buying your second and third courses.

In Chapter One, I asked you to look beyond the course you'll soon be making and think of the bigger picture. Your online course business.

Thinking in terms of your business allows you to think long-term.

Your priorities change.

When you think in terms of what's best for your business, your priorities shift. They go from creating an online course and selling it to as many people as possible to creating a streamlined business and brand that delivers real value to its audience and fans.

If that's the sort of efficient business model you want to build, then you must leverage the community you already have.

Don't go about creating a new course in an entirely different niche and building a community from scratch!

If you end up in a situation where you realise your first online course's niche was a poor choice, it's okay to start afresh and find another niche that you're more passionate about. However, you should also recognise that the first course you made will no longer be a part of your brand and business model.

In other words, you'll be starting all over again. The second course you make will now be your first, meaning you must do all the market, content, and audience research right from the very beginning.

What do we mean by "Niche?"

A Niche is a concept or idea intended for specific appeal to the marketplace. It describes the specific audience segment that the content (your course in this case) is created for — based on their interests, habits, and goals.

CREATE YOUR ONLINE COURSE WITH THESE 8 EASY STEPS

Exercise #2

See if you can come up with three course topic ideas. All topics should belong to the same niche and you should have one for each level of online course we discussed.

YOUR NICHE:

Interested Course: ....

Qualified Course: ....

Committed Course: ....

USE THIS CHECKLIST AS YOU GO THROUGH THIS BOOK

- [ ] HAVE YOU CHOSEN A TOPIC FOR YOUR COURSE THAT YOUR PASSIONATE ABOUT AND ABLE TO DEMONSTRATE EXPERTISE IN?

- [ ] HAVE YOU BEEN ABLE TO PROVE THERE IS SUFFICIENT INTEREST (MARKET DEMAND) IN YOUR ONLINE COURSE IDEA?

- [ ] DID YOU CARRY OUT A SURVEY OF 8-20 PEOPLE (YOUR MARKET RESEARCH FOCUS GROUP) AND SUMMARISE THE FINDINGS?

- [ ] HAVE YOU DECIDED THE FORMAT(S) YOU WILL BE USING TO CREATE YOUR COURSE & ANY ADDITIONAL RESOURCES YOU WILL PROVIDE?

- [ ] DID YOU FIND YOUR FIRST & SECOND THESIS PRICE, AND STUDY THE COMPETITION TO UNDERSTAND HOW YOUR COURSE COMPARES?

- [ ] DO YOU HAVE TESTIMONIALS AND REVIEWS THAT YOU CAN USE TO PROMOTE YOUR COURSE TO YOUR AUDIENCE PRE-LAUNCH?

- [ ] ARE YOU GROWING YOUR AUDIENCE EVERYDAY & DIVERSIFYING YOUR REVENUE STREAM OPPORTUNITIES?

GOALS

...setting goals before starting a new project is probably **the best way** of making sure you get anything done!

...the reason being is that goals keep us <u>accountable</u> to ourselves, which is <u>invaluable</u> when we face hurdles we must overcome or feel unmotivated!

...which is why, <u>you need a plan!</u>

CREATE YOUR PLAN TODAY!

1 Write down your long term goals and why these goals matter

2 Think carefully about what you will need to achieve these goals

3 Break down long term goals into achievable short term goals

YOUR GOALS MUST BE S.M.A.R.T!

S.M.A.R.T GOALS

Name _____

Specific 	Specific means that your goal is detailed and exact. It can answer the questions who, what, where, when, why, and which.	
Measurable 	Measurable means you can track your progress and know exactly when your goal is met. It usually involved numbers.	
Attainable 	Attainable means that your goal is a reasonable one. It is not completely out of reach, or too easy for you.	
Relevant 	Relevant means that your goal is worthwhile. It is something that is actually important to you right now.	
Timely 	Timely means that your goal will be accomplished in a set time frame, such as two weeks, three months, or one year.	

- SET GOAL
- MAKE PLAN
- GET TO WORK
- STICK TO IT
- REACH GOAL
- GOOD JOB!

PART II

CHAPTER THREE
"CHOOSE A COURSE TOPIC THAT TICKS ALL THE RIGHT BOXES"

"The difference between something good and something great is attention to detail."
– Charles R Swindoll

Many of you reading this book probably already have a topic in mind for your first online course. You know exactly what you want your first online course to be about. You might even be tempted to skip ahead to the next chapter.

PLEASE. DON'T. DO. THAT.

DON'T. SKIP. AHEAD.

It's no secret that content creators and entrepreneurs get a lot of great ideas all the time. And yet, the vast majority of these ideas don't end up working out in the end.

Why do you think that is? Have a think about it.

More often than not, our best and brightest ideas don't fail because they're bad ideas per se, but because we did not put in the work to test and polish these ideas thoroughly.

This is usually when I like to point my clients to the video streaming giant, Netflix. At its core, Netflix's mission has always been to make video entertainment more accessible to the public. That's what they've always tried to do. That (their mission statement) has never really changed. It's *how* they approach this mission statement that has dramatically shifted and changed over the years.

> ### *A Lesson From History...*
>
> Few people know this, but Netflix was actually founded all the way back in 1997 as one of the first e-commerce websites. Back then, Netflix generated revenue almost exclusively from selling DVDs. A few years later, the company pivoted towards DVD rentals and, later, created a DVD subscription service — all before launching the video-on-demand (VOD) streaming service we know today.
>
> *Why am I telling you all this?*

The point I'm trying to make is that people like you and I don't have the same luxuries Netflix has (seemingly unlimited investor money and many years of trial and error before they finally get it right).

People like us must test and polish our ideas thoroughly before we launch them. If we don't, we risk gambling away our finite time and resources, which we could be investing in more effective ways. You don't want to end in a situation where you realise there is no demand for your online course after having spent hundreds of hours creating your course.

Worse, you don't want to go through all that trouble, only to realise in the end that your approach and angle were just slightly off!

A little time now can save you a lot of heartache down the road.

Read This Next

Wiley's "Testing Business Ideas" is a practical guide, which contains a library of hands-on techniques for rapidly testing new business ideas. 7 out of every 10 new products fail to deliver on expectations.

USE THESE THREE CRITERIA TO SCREEN COURSE IDEAS

Any topic you choose must fulfil all three of the following criteria:
1. must be about something you're genuinely passionate about
2. must be in an area where you have experience and expertise
3. must be something people want to learn about (market demand)

1. Passion

It might sound obvious, but you need to be genuinely passionate about your course topic. In other words, you should fundamentally care and be deeply invested in whatever you choose to teach your students. Too many people make the rookie mistake of creating an online course about a topic they have little or no interest in.

Why do they do this?

Oftentimes, they're simply following the latest trends and targeting the most profitable niches they can find. Essentially, they're only thinking as far along as their first online course and don't realise that this first course will be a part of a broader business model and ecosystem. As a consequence, they end up *"trapping"* themselves in a niche they don't enjoy. Is that the sort of life you envisioned when you imagined your ideal self and life in Chapter One?

Do you really see yourself spending the rest of your life having your soul sucked out because you chose to create content in a niche that neither interests nor inspires you? *No? Good. I didn't think so.*

Creating an online course is an incredibly rewarding experience.

However, it's also challenging and typically involves many months of hard work. It might even turn out to be the hardest and most rewarding thing you've ever accomplished so far! Like any good investment, you will likely need to wait a long time before seeing a substantial return. If you choose a topic you're not passionate about, you're choosing to make your life harder and will find it challenging to stay motivated during the many months it takes to plan, compile, create, produce, launch, and promote your online course.

2. Expertise

Passion alone is not enough, however. You must also be an expert in what you plan to teach your students.

One of the things that we must all acknowledge and accept is that, sometimes, we're well-suited for the role of teacher. Other times, however, we're probably better placed as students.

There is nothing wrong with that. We all have things we can learn from one another. The reason expertise matters is because, without expertise, you'll find it very difficult to establish your credibility with your audience. And, credibility?

It matters... A LOT.

Top Tip Time

It's our credibility that allows us to build trust with our audience and customers, and it's this trust that makes our customers trust us enough to purchase our products and services. Without trust, you'll have a much harder time convincing potential clients to give you their hard-earned money and buy your online course.

When you make any important business decision, it's always good to take a step back and consider how your decision affects your credibility with your audience. This becomes crucial when you launch your online course and other e-learning products and begin negotiating sponsorship deals. **Your credibility is everything.**

Ready for the good news?

You can demonstrate your expertise in a particular niche in many different ways. For example, on my YouTube channel, I create videos explaining how the brain works and the different things that we can all do to enhance its health and performance.

To illustrate to the viewer that I actually know what I'm talking about, I'll introduce myself by name. I'll state that I'm a medical doctor. Tell the viewer that I graduated from the University of Cambridge and that I'm currently training to be a neuropsychiatrist.

This little "bio" helps set me apart from all the other YouTubers who do a similar thing as me but don't have the same professional qualifications. My professional qualifications make my videos more credible and give my audience a reason to watch my content over someone else's. You must know, however, that professional qualifications are not the only way you can illustrate your expertise.

In fact, they're not even the best or most effective way.

Online Course Case Study

I often get asked how I, a medical doctor, got into the e-learning and online course creation space. People are, understandably, surprised to see someone like me in this space.

And... well, it was actually through YouTube!

A few years ago, I was approached by a client on Upwork who was looking for someone to research and script their online course for them. *The problem?* I had just started out on Upwork and had zero reviews on the platform. Understandably, the client was unconvinced that I had the necessary expertise.

I knew I could do it, though.

I told them how I research and script all my YouTube videos myself and sent them links to several of these videos along with the scripts I'd written for them. I made it abundantly clear that, while no one had hired me for a similar gig before, I definitely had the skillset needed. I got the job and still work with that same client today as an external e-learning consultant and have helped them develop several other e-learning products since then.

One thing I hope this story illustrates is that you absolutely do not need formal qualifications to demonstrate expertise.

I never went to scriptwriting school or took any writing courses.

The client hired me because I was able to show the client that I could deliver the results they needed.

Offering tangible proof is, arguably, the most effective way of demonstrating your expertise to potential buyers.

In fact, I believe it's a far better strategy than listing professional qualifications.

Another excellent example is Ali Abdaal.

Abdaal is the creator of the Part-Time YouTuber Academy, a five-week boot camp where aspiring YouTubers learn the secrets to growing their YouTube audience.

As part of the boot camp, students work on projects and obtain feedback, attend weekly live sessions with Abdaal and other guest speakers, and participate in daily live workshops.

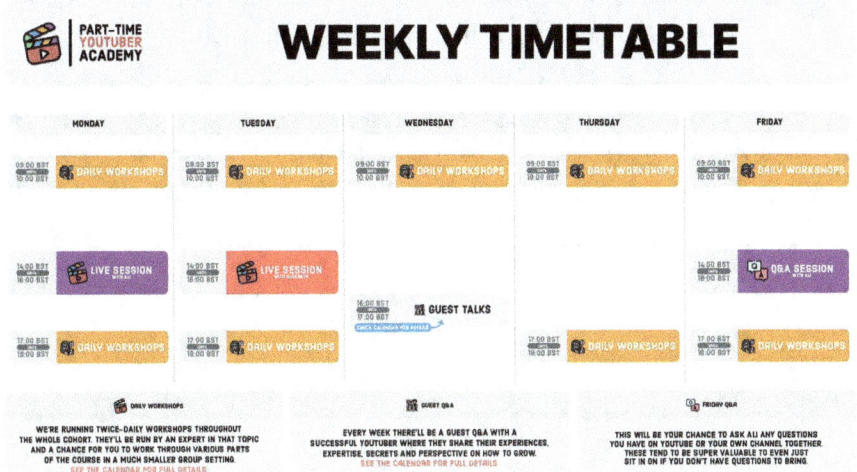

Ali can charge his students between $2,000-$6,000 because of the high degree of support and accountability his course provides.

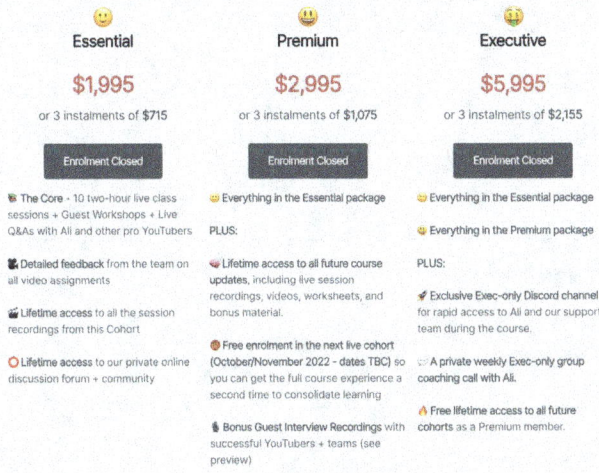

However, another reason Ali can charge this much is because he has credibility and can illustrate his expertise by pointing to his YouTube channel, which today has over 3 million subscribers.

Even better, he can tell potential buyers how he managed to grow his YouTube channel while he worked days and nights as a junior doctor in the United Kingdom. *Ali is the ultimate Part-Time YouTuber.*

If you're going to learn how to become a Part-Time YouTuber (something a lot of people are likely to be interested in), who better to learn it from other than Ali?

Exercise #3

For this exercise, I'd like you to write down at least 4 pieces of evidence that you will use to demonstrate your expertise and credibility to your clients. Keep it brief, but be specific.

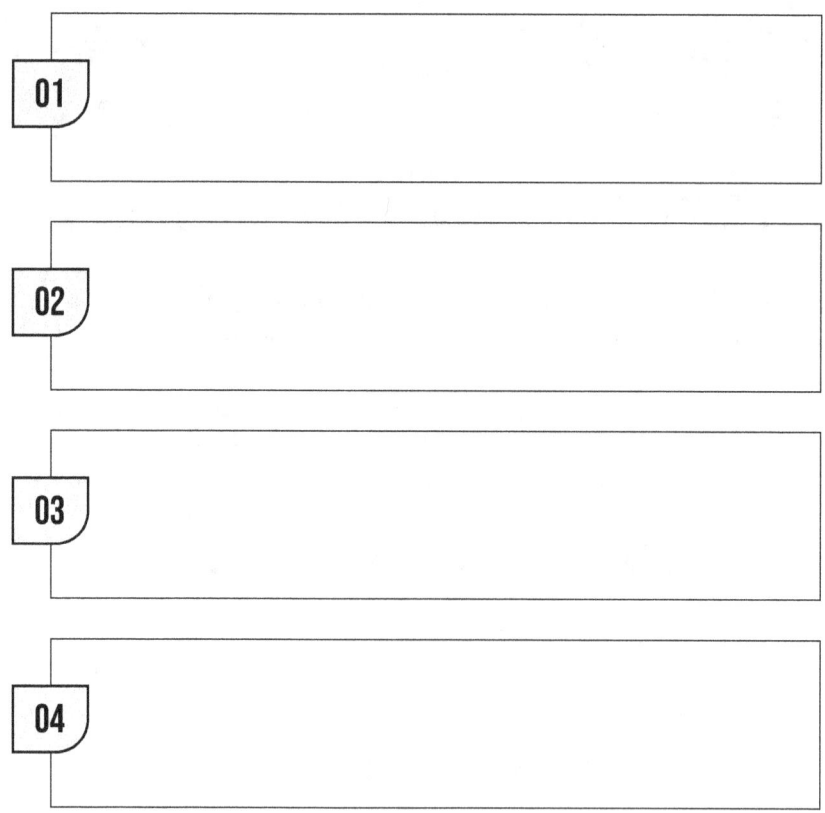

> ### *Top Tip Time*
>
> It's not simply enough to tell potential buyers, "I have a YouTube channel." A lot of people have YouTube channels!
>
> How does that make you credible?
>
> Instead, you should say, "I have a YouTube channel with over 1 million subscribers. I was able to generate nearly $2 million in revenue in 2021. I managed to grow my channel in 2 years and I can teach you how you can do the same." Perfect.

Notice how, in the example above, I used specific "results-driven" language. You should adopt a "results-driven" mindset when you plan and create your online courses. A lot of educators promoting their first course will make the mistake of focusing purely on all the different things their students will learn from them.

While it's certainly a good idea to include a list of learning outcomes on your course website, **you should never lead with it.**

Bear in mind that the vast majority of people who will consider buying your course won't do so for the love of learning. They want to buy your course because they're hoping to do something with the knowledge that you teach them. Just ask yourself;

"Why did you go out of your way to buy this book?"

You most likely purchased this book to use its knowledge to help you create your first online course. I doubt you want to learn all about creating your first online course, just for the sake of it! You're driven by results. So am I.

Your audience is just like you and me.

Their purchase decisions are primarily driven by what they'll be able to do with the knowledge they learn from you.

When approaching your customers, don't lead by telling them about what they will learn but describe to them what they will be able to do and achieve with that knowledge.

Pique their interest.

Once you have their attention, back up your claims with a list of learning outcomes, video lectures, and other resources you plan to include. These will describe the technicalities of what you plan to teach.

If you lead your sales pitch with a results-driven message and then follow it with a description of your course content, you appeal to your customers on both an emotional and rational level.

They'll have absolutely no reason not to buy your course.

You've told them **why they should buy your course** (the results they will achieve) and **how you plan to teach the course**, so they actually achieve those results.

3. Market Demand

Finally, there must also be sufficient market demand for what you plan to teach. A good test I like to use is to ask yourself if your course topic is a million-dollar idea. Now, to be honest, no one expects you to make a million dollars from your first online course.

However, you should potentially be able to.

"So, what's a million-dollar course idea, then?"

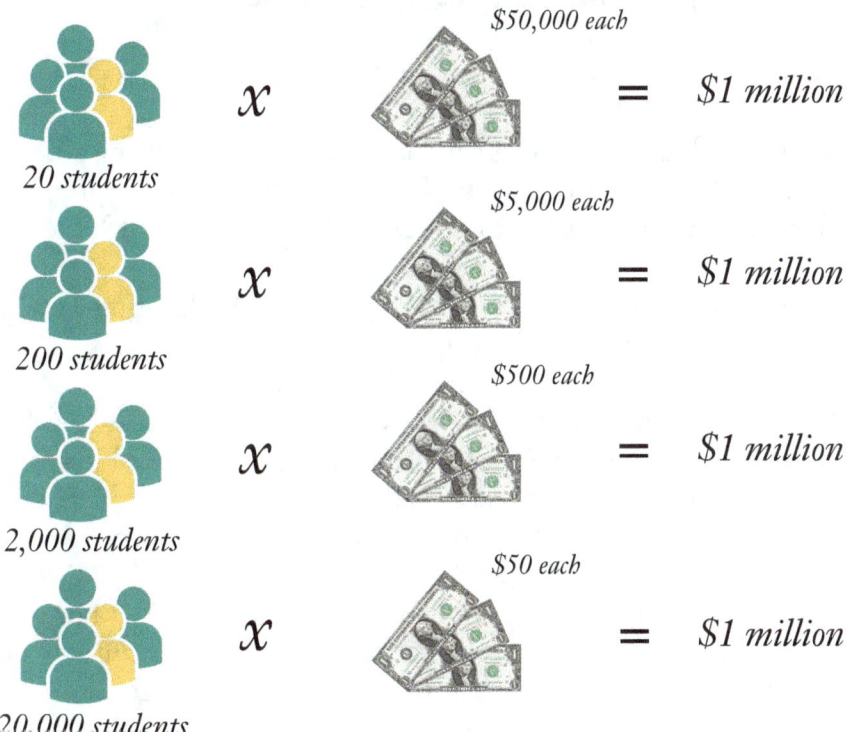

It depends on the level of online course you plan to create.

If you don't think you can realistically find the number of students you need to generate a million dollars from your online course, you should rethink whether or not your course idea is truly viable. Are there enough people interested in learning about this topic?

You can use **Google Trends** and **Google's Keyword Planner** to find if there is market interest. Both tools are free to use and allow you to gauge market interest by uncovering keyword search volumes.

What do we mean by "Keyword Search Volume?"
The Keyword Search Volume is the number of times a specific keyword was searched for on a search engine (like Google) in a given timeframe.

Online Course Case Study

I had a client who was a knitting influencer.

She approached me because she wanted to create a knitting course. She already had 15,000 fans on Instagram she could promote her course to, but she was hoping to expand her reach.

I was honest with her. I'd never worked on a knitting course before. I had no idea if the course topic was really viable.

It was, therefore, crucial we prove there was healthy market demand for her course. And so, using Google's Keyword Planner, we found that people had searched for the keyword *"knitting for beginners"* between 10,000 and 100,000 times each month.

That's a lot of potential customers for an introductory knitting course. We then used Google Trends and found that interest in *"knitting"* tends to peak yearly around the holiday season.

Makes sense, right?

Well, we were able to use this information to determine precisely when the best time to launch the course was. Finally, we went back to Google's Keyword Planner and took a closer look at the analytics. That's when we realised that *"knitting"* was, in fact, a pretty competitive niche market to enter.

SHOULD YOU AVOID COMPETITIVE NICHES?

A competitive niche is one where there are lots of other people trying to do the same thing you're trying to do. During your market research, you might realise that your chosen course topic belongs in a competitive niche. Does this mean you should quit and find another less competitive niche? *Maybe. Maybe not.*

It all depends on your approach. There are no hard rules here.

A non-competitive niche will usually be non-competitive because there isn't much demand for it. While high demand, non-competitive niches certainly exist, they are often hard to come by. If you find them, your *"discoverer"* advantage will quickly erode as other course creators flock to create their own courses on the same topic.

It's, therefore, easiest to consider the two realistic choices we have.

- Choose a smaller, less competitive market/niche
- Choose a larger, more competitive market/niche

Smaller, Less Competitive	*Larger, More Competitive*
If you choose this market, you must accept that, in all likelihood, there will be a hard ceiling beyond which your business will not grow. While the growth of your business may be stunted in the future, your life will be easier as you face less competition and your target audience is easier to find and recruit to your community.	If you choose this market, you need to stand out from the crowd. You can't just simply offer a high quality product because there are dozens of other similar good products out there already. You'll need something else that makes both you and your online course special. A "secret sauce" if you like.

Formally, I'd call this *"differentiating yourself from the competition."*

It's the art and science of standing out.

There are two main ways you can do this.

CONTENT TILT

This is when you create a niche within a niche for your online course business. Sometimes, it involves finding the overlap between two high-demand competitive niches.

This overlap becomes your market opportunity.

For example, instead of teaching people to knit, you'll teach them how to knit "impossible" patterns.

PERSONAL TILT

This is when you make yourself stand out from the crowd through sheer charisma and personality.

You might insert a joke here and there. You might make people laugh. People think you're interesting and they're drawn to you.

Best of all is if you're able to use your personality to teach your course in smart and innovative ways.

Exercise #4

Can you think of any content creators (course instructors, YouTubers, and Podcasters) who make use of "Personal Tilt" in their content? How do they do it?

WHAT IF YOU DON'T HAVE ANY IDEAS FOR A COURSE TOPIC?

If you're feeling lost for ideas but know that you want to create an online course, fear not! My recommendation is that you make a list of 30 things that you're genuinely passionate about.

On that list, include:
- Any Hobbies & Interests You Have
- What You Talk About With Friends
- Stuff You Read About For Leisure
- Accounts You Follow On Social Media

If you do this exercise with care and patience, you might discover something new about yourself that you didn't know before!

A friend of mine, for example, realised that everyone in our friend group was always going to him for relationship advice. He was some sort of unofficial dating guru/coach.

Eventually, he "tapped" into this potential and monetised it by creating an online course where he taught people (mainly young and single men) how to date. Before he went ahead and created that course, however, he did do his due diligence by carefully researching and studying the market opportunity. In fact, it was through market research that he narrowed down his audience to target young and single men. The message here is that, with enough ingenuity, you can monetise practically anything that you enjoy doing. Once you have a list of things you enjoy, go through each item and assess your expertise in that field and the size of the opportunity.

Create a shortlist once you're done.

If you're still stuck, visit an online course marketplace for inspiration. These websites include Udemy, Teachable, and Skillshare. Udemy, in fact, has a free search tool on its website that lets you find what courses students are looking for right now.

Exercise #5

Use this exercise to come up with a list of 10 things that you're passionate about. For each item, assess your expertise and the market demand. Finally, create a short list.

	Topic Idea	Expertise?	Market Demand?
1.		○	○
2.		○	○
3.		○	○
4.		○	○
5.		○	○
6.		○	○
7.		○	○
8.		○	○
9.		○	○
10.		○	○

Short List

1.
2.
3.

START YOUR ONLINE COURSE BUSINESS TODAY

Exercise #6

Once you've decided on your niche and a topic for your online course, I want you to pay a visit to Udemy and find the 3 most successful course creators in your niche.

Course Creator's Name

Niche

Name Of Course Offered #1

Name Of Course Offered #2

- *What do these course creators offer in their courses that sets them apart from their competition?*

Name Of Course Offered #3

- *What positive things do the reviews say about this instructor's courses?*

- *What negative things do the reviews say about this instructor's courses?*

PROFILE 1

39

PROFILE 2

PROFILE 3

You should always consider your audience first and foremost and prioritise their needs above all else. A course that's more suited to the viewer's needs will perform better than its competition.

This will reflect in your sales, reviews, and testimonials, which is precisely why you must spend some time studying the courses that your competitors offer. Identify the things that these courses did well **(so you can do more of them)** and the things that these courses did poorly **(so you can avoid or do them differently)**.

Before you commit to any topic, the safest approach would be for you to host a free webinar or online workshop to gauge market interest in your course. You can even charge those attending a small symbolic fee! When you charge a small fee, you establish market interest and also confirm that there are indeed people out there willing to pay to learn about this topic from you.

Furthermore, hosting a webinar or workshop will allow you to connect with your audience and potential clients. You can start growing your mailing list and building your community long before you launch your online course. These workshop attendees become a part of your "beta test group" and can help you in your course creation process by offering you valuable feedback.

After the workshop, you should ask the attendees the following:

"Did you enjoy my teaching style?"

"What was the one thing you liked most about the workshop?"

"What was the one thing you liked least about the workshop?"

"Is there anything I didn't cover that you wish I had?"

"Would you pay for a full and more comprehensive online course?"

"How much would you be willing to pay?"

8 BEST KEYWORD RESEARCH TOOLS

Google Trends	Explore and analyze real time and historial search trends from different locations.
QuestionDB	Leverage questions people are asking on websites and forums like Reddit.
AnswerThePublic	Use data from Google autocomplete to find long tail keywords.
TubeBuddy	Use this browser extension to access YouTube keyword data and manage your channel.
Keyword Tool	Access Google autocomplete data from a variety of search engines, from Google to Amazon.
Also Asked	Use Google's People Also Ask data to perform keyword research related to your business.
Soovle	Quickly compare related search suggestions across many different search platforms.
Google Ads	Use Keyword Planner to research keyword ideas for your paid search campaigns.

PART II

CHAPTER FOUR

"DEVELOP A COURSE OUTLINE FROM YOUR COURSE TOPIC"

"Brainstorming is the nexus of ideas."
– Asa Don Brown

Once you've identified the topic you want your course to be about, the next step will be to turn this idea into a course outline. The course outline expands on your initial idea, turning that idea into a short list of ideas that later become your course modules. It's essentially the framework that will carry you through your journey from start to finish.

It gives you a detailed plan to follow so you feel more grounded and confident when creating your first online course.

> More often than not, our best and brightest ideas don't fail because they're bad ideas per se, but because we did not put in the work to test and polish these ideas thoroughly.

Start creating your course outline by breaking down your course topic into three to six concepts you plan to teach your students. You should choose these concepts according to your audience's needs. What you teach your students should align with your market research and the feedback you receive from your target audience and beta test group.

> The better you understand the needs of your audience, the more likely you will be able to satisfy those needs – and the more successful your online course and business will be.

Using Google Ads' Keyword Planner and AnswerThePublic, you'll be able to see precisely what questions are being asked by your target audience about your chosen topic.

For example, suppose you're creating an online course on "Productivity" and "Overcoming Procrastination." Using the tools mentioned above, you'll find that some of the most popular search terms include "productivity meaning" "productivity planner" "chronic procrastination" "toxic productivity," and "time management matrix." If these are the keywords people search for the most, it's likely that these are keywords your audience wants to learn more about. You should seriously consider using these search terms in your course outline.

Here's an example of what a five-part course outline on overcoming procrastination that makes use of these search terms would look like:

1. *Are you a chronic procrastinator? What is procrastination?*
2. *How can we manage our time to maximise our productivity?*
3. *What is a time management matrix? How can you use it?*
4. *Can productivity ever be toxic?*
5. *How can you avoid toxic productivity?*

However, what's even better than sitting behind a computer screen and looking at analytics is connecting directly with your customers and asking them what they want to learn about a particular topic. After all, there may be a lot that your students can learn from you, but there is still so much that your students can teach you!

In fact, as content creators and business owners, we often get some of our brightest ideas from our audience.

That's why you need a market research focus group.

Setting up a market research focus group may seem a little overwhelming if you're creating your first online course and don't have an audience to reach out to (yet). I promise it's nowhere nearly as difficult as it seems! You only need eight to twenty people who belong to your target audience. *Doesn't sound too bad, does it?*

To find these eight to twenty people, you'll first need to find where your target audience spends their time online learning about your chosen topic or niche. The fact is your target customers likely already have a keen interest in the subject you plan to teach them.

You probably won't be introducing them to this topic.

They're getting their "fix" from somewhere.

Find out where that place is.

Personally, my favourite place to find interested customers is through Reddit. As Reddit's communities are interest-based, finding the right community for your niche and topic should be easy.

Other popular alternatives to Reddit include Discord, Twitter, Substack, LinkedIn and Facebook groups. These are all excellent places where you can meet your future students, build valuable relationships, and begin growing your audience and network.

> *"Time on social media is not time wasted,
> but it's time invested."*

Most content creators with something to sell or promote will spend far too much time pushing their products and services to clients and too little time engaging with their clients — as people.

Don't be one of those creators.

Doing business like this will, in the long run, do more damage than good to your credibility, business, and personal brand.

After all, people want nothing more than to be treated as people, which means you should value and respect your audience for more than what they can do for your bottom line.

01 When you first join an online space, understand that this isn't your space (yet). It's someone else's space, meaning you must treat it respectfully. For now, you're nothing more than a guest.

02 Don't spam your clients. Don't promote your course, brand, and other products right away. Absolutely don't do that. People will see right through and dislike you.

03 Spend your time learning the unspoken rules and subtleties of each platform and online community. For example, behaviour that's acceptable on Facebook may be unacceptable on Reddit.

04 Every week, make a list of all the popular and trending posts in that community, until you know your target audience inside out and understand their likes, dislikes, and interests.

05 Once you're comfortable with the community's unspoken rules, leverage your expertise to answer questions and solve problems for your customers — free of charge! Build trust first, monetise later.

Offering value first, before making your sales pitch, is the most important thing you can do create trust and establish credibility.

There is no such thing as a free lunch.

You must first engage, offer value, and pay your dues, before you make your sales pitch.

The best part? You get to prove your expertise without having to broadcast and boast about all your accomplishments and credentials, which some people may, understandably, find off-putting.

Furthermore, it will make it incredibly easy to find the eight to twenty people you need for your market research focus group. Because you've helped them in the past and answered their questions, your target audience will jump at the chance to help you create your e-learning product and course offering.

Once you've earned your audience's respect, they'll be more than happy to help you with your market research.

Top Tip Time

You might also find it helpful to sweeten the deal a little by putting together a free guide or manual to send to anyone who completes your market survey. This costs you nothing and can help you get in touch with many of your interested customers.

Once you have your focus group ready,
ask each survey participant the following six questions:

- *What are the biggest challenges you face about [INSERT TOPIC]?*
- *What are your biggest fears and frustrations about [INSERT TOPIC]?*
- *What do you want to learn about [INSERT TOPIC]?*
- *What do you want to do with what you've learnt about [INSERT TOPIC]?*
- *What would you like to see offered in an online course package?*
- *How much would you be willing to pay for the package described above?*

You should now be able to create a thorough and robust course outline using all the information you collected from:

- researching keywords and market analytics data
- observing your target audience and their interactions with each other in online forums and communities
- carrying out the market research focus group questionnaire

That said, you will still need to find a way to connect your key ideas together so that they not only inform/educate your students but also create a cohesive narrative for your students to follow and become invested in. Storytelling is crucial, and your course must "flow" to keep your audiences engaged from start to finish.

> ### *Top Tip Time*
>
> Don't ever underestimate the power of narrative. You may not be a novelist, but you're still a content creator, and nearly all good content revolves around good storytelling. This includes the educational content you create for your online course.

Read This Next

In The Science of Storytelling, psychological research and cutting-edge neuroscience are used to show us how we can write better stories, revealing how storytellers and their brains can create engaging worlds.

Read This Next

"Storytelling With Data" teaches you the fundamentals of data visualization and how to communicate effectively with data. You'll discover the power of storytelling and the way to make data a pivotal point in your story.

 *If you don't have time to read those books, I don't blame you.*

I barely have any time to read myself! Sign up to my mailing list to be the first to know when I publish a summary of the two storytelling books above.

If one of the key ideas you came up with doesn't feel like it belongs with the other ideas you have written down, unless it's absolutely essential, consider cutting it out. Don't fall into the trap of trying to include as much information as possible in your online course.

It's not what your students want. It's not what you want.

It's not what anyone wants.

You might believe that overloading your students with everything they might ever need to know about a particular topic makes your course offering more comprehensive and, therefore, better.

This could not be further from the truth.

As mentioned in Chapter Two, your students are primarily buying your course for the support and accountability you offer. It's, therefore, almost always a much better strategy to teach a few valuable lessons well than teach many lessons badly.

When in doubt, go with the proverbial sayings, "less is more" and "quality over quantity." Any ideas that don't make the cut can be saved on your phone for later to be used in the future when you create courses for qualified and committed customers.

Once you have your course outline ready, go back to your focus group and ask them for their feedback on your course outline.

To avoid getting poor quality feedback, don't just ask your customers if they think your outline is "good" or if they "like it." Nine times out of ten, they'll tell you it's "amazing" without offering anything more constructive. Ask your target audience to tell you precisely how they would improve the course outline, the things that they would change, and what they like the most and want to see more of in the course. Feel free to offer incentives, including discounts and access to exclusive bonus content, to the clients who come back to you with the best and most thorough feedback. Handing out "freebies" promotes loyalty and creates superfans for your work who feel valued and become actively involved in your brand.

When the time comes, your superfans will be the ones who will do much of the heavy lifting for you.

They'll spread your message and promote your course, enabling you to scale up your business much more rapidly.

SUPERFANS

Exercise #7

It's now time to use all the information you've gathered so far to create a mission statement for your first online course and your e-learning business!

You mission statement should only include 3 things:

- [ ] Who your target audience is, or who this course is intended for

- [ ] What you plan to teach your students in the course

- [ ] What your students will be able to achieve after taking the course

EXAMPLE

> **MISSION STATEMENT**
>
> "Welcome to the Online Filmmaking School. My online courses teach budding filmmakers all the basics of filmmaking so they can go on to create their first short film and begin their professional film careers."

Word Count = 34 words

YOUR TURN

> **MISSION STATEMENT**
>
>

Keep It Simple. Keep It Brief.

3
THE GRIND

PART III

CHAPTER FIVE

"HOW TO CREATE ENGAGING MATERIAL FOR YOUR ONLINE COURSE"

"We need to stop interrupting what people are interested in and be what people are interested in."
– Craig Davis

One of the questions I told you to ask your market research focus group in Chapter Three was as follows; *"What would you like to see offered in an online course package about this topic?"*

The answers you receive to this question will help inform you of the best way to deliver the course content to your students.

Once you've broken down your course topic into a course outline with all your course modules written down, it'll be time to break down these modules further into individual video lectures.

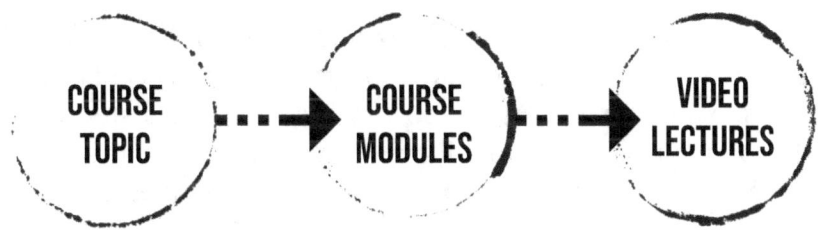

I think the best way to plan an online course is to think in terms of the intended learning outcomes (ILOs).

Think of each lecture you're planning to create for your students in terms of what the student will have learnt after having watched it. These are your learning outcomes. Write them down in bullet point form and keep them in mind when you're creating content for your online course. Ideally, each video lecture should have no more than three bullet points/learning outcomes underneath it. If it has more than three, you should consider splitting the lecture into two.

> ### *Top Tip Time*
> People's attention spans are getting shorter, which is why you should keep each video lecture as brief and self-contained as possible. Generally, I advise that each lesson be between 6-8 minutes long and no longer than 10 minutes long.
>
> Studies show that online content that is 3-7 minutes long boosts learning and spontaneous fact retention by at least 17%.

Furthermore, once you've written down one to three learning outcomes underneath each of your video lectures, save that list.

You can use that list once you launch your course to give your students something they're able to use to track their progress. A checklist of sorts that will be one more feature you can add to your course to enhance its value, for just a little extra work on your end.

For now, however, you'll need to go through these learning outcomes yourself and ask "what's the most effective way to teach this concept so my students get the most value from my lesson(s)?"

Sometimes the best way to teach something will be to create video footage where you describe and explain the key concepts to your students. You may also use video footage to create a step-by-step guide for your students to follow. Other times, the best way to teach a particular topic/concept will be through PowerPoint slides and colourful handouts that your students can read now and access later if and when they need to. Courses for qualified and committed customers will also include one-on-one time with the instructor, live Q&A sessions, quizzes, and class projects/assignments.

Exercise #8; Types Of E-Learning Content
Go through the list and familiarise yourself with the different types of e-learning content you can create. Use the check boxes to decide if you want to create this content.

- [ ] **ARTICLES**
- [ ] **ANIMATED GIFs**
- [ ] **BLOG POSTS**
- [ ] **ASSESSMENTS**
- [ ] **CASE STUDIES**
- [ ] **WORKBOOKS**
- [ ] **CHECKLISTS**
- [ ] **ILLUSTRATIONS**
- [ ] **INTERVIEWS**
- [ ] **GAMES**
- [ ] **INFOGRAPHICS**
- [ ] **PODCASTS**
- [ ] **POWERPOINTS**
- [ ] **VIDEO LECTURES**
- [ ] **LIVE WEBINARS**
- [ ] **GROUP PROJECTS**

The best online courses will be the ones that don't take a one size fits all approach. You want to use a combination of different formats and select the most appropriate format for each thing you intend to teach.

In addition, using a variety of formats keeps the viewer engaged with your course, so they finish it and feel that they've gotten their money's worth. If they feel they've gotten their money's worth from your course, they'll come back in the future to buy more of your online courses.

However, as you're only just creating your first online course, don't try to run before you can walk. My recommendation is to focus on doing just one or two things and do those things well. For example, if you're creating your first online course for interested customers, you may consider making a course with the following format:

- **[X] hours of video lecture content + bullet point summary handout + course and module checklist**

    ...priced at $25-100 per student

If, on the other hand, you're creating a course for qualified customers, you will want to add more value to justify the cost:

- **[X] hours of video lecture content + bullet point summary handout + course and module checklist +/- exercise/activity workbook +/- weekly live Q&A sessions +/- group projects**

    ...priced at $200-1000 per student

Meanwhile, nothing is off the table if you're working with a committed customer. You will likely find yourself working with them one-on-one to create **a fully customised experience.**

You should, however, bear in mind that the value you deliver to your committed customer must be directly tied to the compensation you receive from them. In other words, don't allow people take advantage of you, your expertise, and your time.

Know Your Worth.

START YOUR ONLINE COURSE BUSINESS TODAY

In the summer of 2022, Taylor Swift delivered the commencement speech at New York University's graduation ceremony. Overall, it was a great speech, and Swift spoke eloquently for 20 minutes!

I remember seeing online conversations about the speech, and I was amazed at the number of people who believed that Taylor Swift had improvised the whole thing! I'm a Swiftie myself, so I 100% believe that Swift is great, but I don't think she's THAT great.

No one is that great.

She clearly scripted the speech beforehand, spent a few good hours rehearsing the speech, and then used **a teleprompter** to deliver the speech at the live graduation ceremony. In fact, I think I could count three different teleprompters that Swift was using.

Taylor Swift isn't special in this regard.

Most people who create video content (course creators, YouTubers, and TikTok and Instagram influencers) script all their videos before recording them. **That's because recording from a script often yields superior outcomes to improvising in front of a camera.**

For starters, you sound a lot more confident because you don't need to worry about what you'll say next. It's right there in front of you! You can focus purely on your style and delivery.

Furthermore, scripting your videos before you record them allows you to edit, *edit, edit, and edit some more* — ensuring that the concepts you teach in your lessons are explained as effectively and as clearly as possible. It cuts down on unnecessary filler. In its place, you can add hooks, metaphors, insightful examples, and other language and storytelling devices that engage your audience.

> Scripting is superior to improvising because it allows you to perfect what you say and how you say it.

I've created online course scripts for many clients, and I almost always use the same template for scriptwriting as the one shown on the next page. You can download an editable Microsoft Word version of this template for free by visiting my website.

The first column is for your script, which we split into manageable "chunks" using the rows in the table as shown. These rows will tell us when to start, pause, and stop speaking. No one actually expects you to deliver a 6-10 minute "speech" all in one go, and you're allowed to take breaks between each bit of text.

The more experienced you get at reading from a teleprompter, the longer you'll be able to read uninterrupted. As a starting point, however, I recommend you keep each chunk to 100-150 words max

VIDEO SCRIPT	VIDEO #

VIDEO TITLE	[Topic]				
KEYWORDS & AUDIENCE		RUNTIME		WRITER	HESHAM M. MASHHOUR
		WORD COUNT			
		EDITOR			

Concepts Covered:	1. SECTION 1 – 2. SECTION 2 – 3. SECTION 3 – 4. SECTION 4 –

	NARRATION	VISUAL CUES	SFX
		I – [PLACEHOLDER]	
1			
2			
3			
4			
5			
6			
7			
8			
9			
10			
11			

— that's around 40-60 seconds of speaking time.

In the second column, we add any visual cues we need to use.

These include the diagrams, illustrations, and stock footage that help explain the various concepts you're describing in the narration. Finally, we write down any visual or sound effects we wish to include in the third column and tidy it up a little. You end up with a *"crib sheet"* that looks something like the document on the right.

Personally, I like using green font for A-Roll (footage of you speaking directly at the camera) and black font for B-Roll (supplementary visuals), but you're obviously free to use any colours you like.

HIRING FREELANCERS

No one is great at everything. There is no shame in admitting that. Each one of us has a unique set of talents, meaning it's often necessary to hire external help. Sometimes, we hire external help even though we can do the task. *Why do we do that?*

It, in fact, ties into one of the most important lessons that Ali Abdaal teaches in his YouTube Part-Time Academy.

You need to understand that your time is your most valuable asset. Invest it wisely to maximise your overall returns. What I mean when I say this is that your time is a very precious and limited resource. If you believe you can get better outcomes/returns by spending that time doing something else, you should delegate the responsibility for that task. Outsourcing has become a cornerstone of the content creation process, and you must find out how to incorporate it into your online course business model.

If you have the financial means to do so, find someone to do the time-consuming things you don't enjoy doing, so you can focus

NEURON THEORY

Video:	WHY VIRTUAL REALITY AND THE METAVERSE ARE THE FUTURE OF MENTAL HEALTH (TREATMENT)	Runtime:	~10 minutes (I PROMISE, I USED A CALCULATOR)	Writer:	HESHAM MASHHOUR
		Word Count:	1453 words	Editor:	MOHAMED SAMAK

NOTES
- SFX were REALLY LOUD last time, let's take it down a little (because you couldn't hear me over the sfx)
- I'm not sure about the fonts used, I think we need a more solid font (look below)
- If you can think of a better idea for a standardised background 1, go for it (just run it by me first)

#	NARRATION	VISUAL CUES	EFFECTS
1	Critics of the metaverse are worried about the potential impact virtual reality could have on the mental health and well-being of its users.	IMAGE 1 [EDIT TO BE DARKER] INSERT TEXT "METAVERSE" w/DYNAMIC ZOOM [SOMETHING LIKE THIS... I ALSO THINK THIS FONT AND LOOK IS PERFECT]	SCIFI HORROR SFX BEGINS AND CONTINUES FOR SEGMENTS 1 & 2 BUT I'M NOT SURE IF IT'S SUCH A GOOD IDEA TO START WITH A SOUND EFFECT...? WHAT DO YOU THINK?
2	Some psychologists have even gone as far as claim that the metaverse's impact on mental health would be nothing short of "devastating;" warning of an impending global psychosis outbreak. [1]	SCREENSHOT 1 w/SOME COOL ANIMATION + HIGHLIGHT "DEVESTATING IMPACT"	(EITHER WAY, PLEASE KEEP THE VOLUME LOW ☺)
3	To be honest, this feels like fearmongering to me. I say this, because to this day no clinical study exists which even remotely supports this idea.	SOME COOL ANIMATION AT "FEARMONGERING"	SAD TRAMBOLINE SFX AT "FEARMONGERING"
4	The idea that the widespread adoption of metaverse technologies is somehow going to lead to more people experiencing more psychotic symptoms.	BASICALLY, TEXT AGAINST BLACK SCREEN METAVERSE ADOPTION =/= MASS PSYCHOSIS w/SOME COOL SHAKING ANIMATION? [SOMETHING LIKE THIS...]	

WHY VIRTUAL REALITY AND THE METAVERSE ARE THE FUTURE OF MENTAL HEALTH (TREATMENT)

instead on doing the things that really matter.

Rome wasn't built in a day.

It wasn't built by a single person, either.

Lucky for content creators like ourselves, there are several outstanding online services available that can help us find the right kind of help. These include Fiverr, Upwork, and TextBroker.

Freelancers on these platforms offer services on everything from topic research and scriptwriting to video editing and content promotion. You'll be able to see what kind of projects each freelancer has worked on in the past and the reviews they've received from their customers.

Moreover, any payments made through these websites will be held in escrow before being released to the freelancer, offering buyers a degree of security. If you're unhappy with the service you received, you can file a complaint and will likely be refunded.

Here are some tips if you choose to hire a freelancer for your course:

- **Hire the right freelancer for the task.** While this may seem obvious, many people think that all writers are the same! The reality is that there are copywriters, technical writers, scriptwriters, research assistants, and editors. These freelance writers will all work very differently and produce considerably different kinds of content.
- **There will often be an initial steep learning curve when you work with someone for the first time.** You will need to communicate your needs to the freelancer clearly. If you don't do that, you'll likely be disappointed in the work they produce. You might even end up wasting more time asking for edits and adjustments.
- **The longer you work with the same person, the more accustomed they become to your preferences.** This means that, over time, you should expect the work

that the freelancer submits to be more aligned with your needs. Therefore, once you find the right freelancers to work with, you should take steps to develop and foster your relationships with them.
- **Tell the freelancer what your goals are for the content they're producing and your overall project.** Communication with your freelancer is paramount to your success. It's your job to provide the freelancer you hire with everything they need to create good and fully customised content that's tailored to your needs.
- **Set the parameters for your project to avoid any unwanted surprises.** This means you must make your expectations apparent. Be specific. Exactly how long do you want your video script to be, how much is your budget, and when do you expect the project done?

If you're working with a freelancer for the first time, I recommend you start by giving them a small piece of work first (one video, for example). Once you're happy with the work they delivered, you can give them larger batches of work.

If you've found a freelancer you like working with, you should move your business with them "off" Fiverr or Upwork and turn them into a regular contractor. This arrangement works well if you have a larger project (like an online course) and can be more cost-effective for both parties. Fiverr, for example, charges a 25% premium.

Top Tip Time

You will usually get what you pay for. If you find a freelancer who charges significantly more for a service than the market average and can still attract customers, there will probably be good reason for this. The service they provide is likely of a higher quality and, therefore, it justifies the price point.

Similarly, freelancers who charge less for the same service can only do so because they'll spend less time on your project and will likely deliver lower-quality uncustomised content.

USE THIS CHECKLIST WHEN HIRING A FREELANCER

- [ ] DOES THE FREELANCER HAVE THE SKILLS NEEDED? HAVE YOU SEEN EXAMPLES OF THEIR PREVIOUS WORK?

- [ ] DOES THE FREELANCER HAVE THE HARDWARE AND SOFTWARE REQUIREMENTS TO COMPLETE THE PROJECT?

- [ ] IS THE FREELANCER PROFESSIONAL IN THEIR COMMUNICATION? DO YOU SEE THEM AS SOMEONE YOU CAN WORK WITH?

- [ ] IS THE FREELANCER ORGANISED AND DO THEY HAVE A HISTORY OF COMPLETING SIMILAR PROJECTS IN A TIMELY MANNER?

- [ ] CAN THE FREELANCER ADD VALUE TO YOUR PROJECT AND ORIGINAL INSIGHT TO DELIVER A CUSTOMISED PRODUCT?

- [ ] HAS THE FREELANCER RECEIVED CLEAR COMMUNICATION FROM YOU ON THE PROJECT GOALS AND EXPECTATIONS?

- [ ] HAVE YOU SENT THE FREELANCER REFERENCES TO GUIDE THEM ON YOUR PREFERENCES FOR THE PROJECT'S VOICE, STYLE & TONE?

- [ ] HAS A BUDGET & PAYMENT SCHEDULE BEEN AGREED ON? HAVE YOU AGREED ON A SUBMISSION DATE?

- [ ] HAVE YOU AGREED WITH THE FREELANCER ON HOW THEY WILL SUBMIT YOUR PROJECT & WHEN THEY WILL DO SO?

- [ ] HAS THE FREELANCER SIGNED ALL CONTRACTS, DOCUMENTS & NON-DISCLOSURE (NDA) AGREEMENTS?

TIPS IF YOU PLAN TO SCRIPT YOUR OWN E-LEARNING VIDEOS

1 Define Your Goals For Each Lesson You Script
- Who are my audience?
- What is my goal?
- How will I achieve my goal?
- What value will it provide?

2 Create An Engaging Narrative For Viewers
- Use anecdotes as "hooks"
- Focus on one single message
- Script as a conversation
- Ask questions to "engage"

3 Cut, Cut, Cut, Cut Edit, Edit, Edit, Edit
- A purpose for every sentence
- Irrelevant sentences removed
- Edit long, complex sentences
- Clear, well-explained concepts

4 Think Like Your Audience Thinks
- Will they understand this?
- Is this relevant to them?
- Is the vocabulary OK?
- Can I get feedback on this?

5 Read The Script Out Loud Before Filming
- You need to know how it sounds
- You can learn to pace yourself
- Get more comfortable with the script
- "Re-script" before filming (if needed)

YOUR TECHNOLOGY NEEDS

Most courses will use video and audio elements to enhance the learning experience, creating a need for technology devices.

A rookie mistake, however, is to go out and spend a whole load of money on a bunch of new and expensive gadgets you don't need!

Here's a list of everything you actually need:

- **A Camera.** You can use your smartphone camera for this! I use my iPhone 12 Pro Max to record all footage for my videos, and I get some excellent-quality footage! Don't spend money on a new camera if you have a smartphone.
- **A Tripod.** While this is something that some people overlook, it will certainly offer you a degree of flexibility when you record your videos, as you won't have to struggle to prop up your camera and teleprompter.
- **A Recording App.** Applications like FiLMiC Pro give you many of the same functionalities on your phone that you can expect to find on a high-end DSLR.
- **A Second Device.** This is used to project your script on the teleprompter. You can use an iPad or tablet for this.
- **A Teleprompter App.** An app that allows you to format your script, adjust the speed, and control the iPad remotely.
- **A Teleprompter.** Teleprompters are very basic pieces of equipment and should be inexpensive to buy. My only real piece of advice here is to remember that a teleprompter will reflect your script from a second screen, like a tablet or a large smartphone. Therefore, the size of your second device dictates the size of your teleprompter.
- **A Microphone.** Almost everyone agrees that you need a high-quality microphone if your students are to understand everything you say! Unfortunately, while

smartphone cameras have advanced considerably in recent years, the same cannot be said for smartphone microphones. I recommend buying a separate microphone. I use a Samson G-Track Pro.

And that's it! You may consider investing in a greenscreen if you want to change the background of your videos. An external lighting system will also afford you the freedom to record your videos at any time during the day. Remember that you cannot use a greenscreen and virtual background without having proper lighting first.

> *Top Tip Time*
>
> Even if you buy the most expensive microphone, you will still need to record your audio in a "sound-friendly" room where noise and echo from hard surfaces are kept to a minimum.
>
> After all, there is only so much that "post" can fix.
>
> Just like a high-end car, you won't get what you're paying for, if you don't know how to use the microphone and record audio.

FOUR LEVELS OF MICROPHONES

Professional Grade Lavalier Lapel Microphone

Vocal Dynamic XLR Microphone for Broadcast

Universal On-Camera Shotgun Vlogging Microphone

Professional USB Condenser Microphone

Click the images to be redirected to Amazon!

Once your footage is ready, you will need to edit this footage. Whether you want to do this yourself or hire someone else to do it for you is entirely up to you. When I was first starting out, I edited all my videos myself. It was hard work but also an incredibly rewarding experience as I learnt new and valuable skills.

However, while video editing is something you can learn to do if you want to keep your costs down, it is also incredibly time-consuming.

That's why I eventually had to hire a video editor as I started making more content, and my time became more valuable.

Either way, I recommend you have a basic working knowledge of how video editing works so you have realistic expectations and can communicate your needs clearly to your video editor.

PART III

CHAPTER SIX

"HOW TO PRICE YOUR ONLINE COURSE TO MAXIMISE REVENUE"

> *"If you do something for fun and create the best possible product, then the profit will come."*
> *– Richard Branson*

When deciding how much you should charge for your course, remember that the price must reflect your course's value. **The more value you add to your course, the more you can charge your clients.** That's the principle all online course creators must use to arrive at the **first thesis price.**

Think of each piece of content that you prepared for your course and the value it provides. How much is each piece of content worth?

Use some of your market research and customer interviews to guide your instincts. For example, as part of your market research, you may remember asking your target audience;

> *"How much would you be willing to pay for the package you described above?"*

The responses you receive from your market research focus group inform your judgement.

If the majority of responses you received were somewhere in the region of $100-$200, it makes little sense to charge $500 for your course. Of course, this is only true if you delivered the same exact package you discussed with your focus group — neither more nor less. If you change your offering, you can no longer rely on the responses you received from your focus group to guide your pricing. **It's also important you realise that we (as content creators) don't exist in isolation, nor do the products we produce.**

Value is not absolute. It's relative.

Online Course Case Study

One of the clients I worked with recently is a talented computer scientist. He recognised that there was an opportunity for him to create an online course about blockchain technology, as it had become very popular over the last few years.

As one of the top talents in his field, he was confident he could teach it as part of an online course. Both he and I expected there to be healthy demand for his Blockchain 101 online course. After all, plenty of people expect blockchain technology to be the future of our computer networks and the internet as a whole.

As an expert who knew his stuff inside out, putting a course together on blockchain technology would be very easy for him. Did that mean that he should only charge a small fee for his course? **Absolutely not.**

Because value, like beauty, lies in the eye of the beholder. In other words, it is determined by both supply and demand economics.

Your course is unlikely to perform well and get many sales if someone out there is also providing the same material (at the same level of quality) — but for a significantly lower price.

That's why you must always study the competition, their course packages, and how much they charge for those packages, when you price your first online course.

1. Begin by visiting course marketplaces like Udemy, Teachable, and Skillshare. Identify creators in your niche.
2. Find out what material their courses include, how that material is taught, and what additional resources they include in their online course offerings.
3. Finally, check how much these instructors charge for their courses, not forgetting to consider any discounts or coupon codes that these creators and educators offer.

The more formats you include in your course and the more interactive your course is, the more you'll be able to sell it for.

Remember that your clients are not buying your course for the knowledge it has but for the learning experience you provide.

> ### *Top Tip Time*
>
> I always encourage my clients to make their courses as interactive as possible. I genuinely believe that interactive content is the future of learning.
>
> Specifically, I'd like to see more course creators in the future offer responsive and interactive booklets, guides, and workbooks.
>
> There are some great platforms online (many of which are free!) that allow you to create and publish responsive/interactive booklets for your students.

Platforms To Create Interactive E-Books
Platforms you can use to create interactive e-books include RockContent, BookBolt, PaperTurn, BookCreator, FlippingBook, Kitaboo, and FlipSnack.

Think hard (and honestly) about how your course stacks up against everything else that's on offer. This is only your first course. Don't expect to have the best or most expensive course out there. The second course you create will undoubtedly be better than your first, and your third will be better than your second. With that in mind, adjust your first thesis price to your **second thesis price.**

ADOPT A DYNAMIC PRICING STRATEGY

Start selling your course at this second thesis price and evaluate how things go from there. Use the sales data and feedback from paying customers to make further adjustments to your pricing.

Your second thesis price will not be your final price, however, and you should expect to fine-tune it into a third, fourth, and even fifth iteration until you eventually find *"the right price."*

But what even is "the right price?"

How do you know when you have found it?

The *"right price"* will be the price where the revenue you generate from the course is at its highest (look at the graph on the right). It is the price that most accurately reflects what your course is worth to your target audience because it strikes a *"perfect"* balance between cost and number of sales.

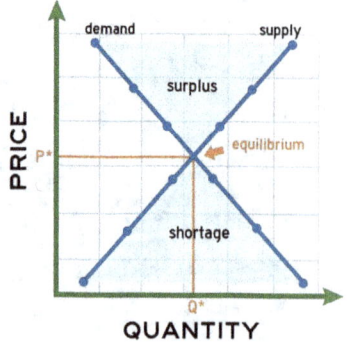

Realistically speaking, some course creators may want to sell their first few online courses at a price point that's *slightly below "the right price."* By selling their course for somewhat less than its market value, these course creators are sacrificing some revenue now in return for more sales, opting for a growth-driven strategy.

It's up to you if you want to adopt it.

It has its pros and cons, and there is no one correct answer.

You're the boss. Only you can decide what's good for you, your business, and your brand. Don't let anyone tell you otherwise.

Exercise #8
It's time you visit course marketplaces and find the cheapest and most expensive courses in your niche. Compare them. How can the expensive course justify their price point, when there is a cheaper alternative out there? Create a list.

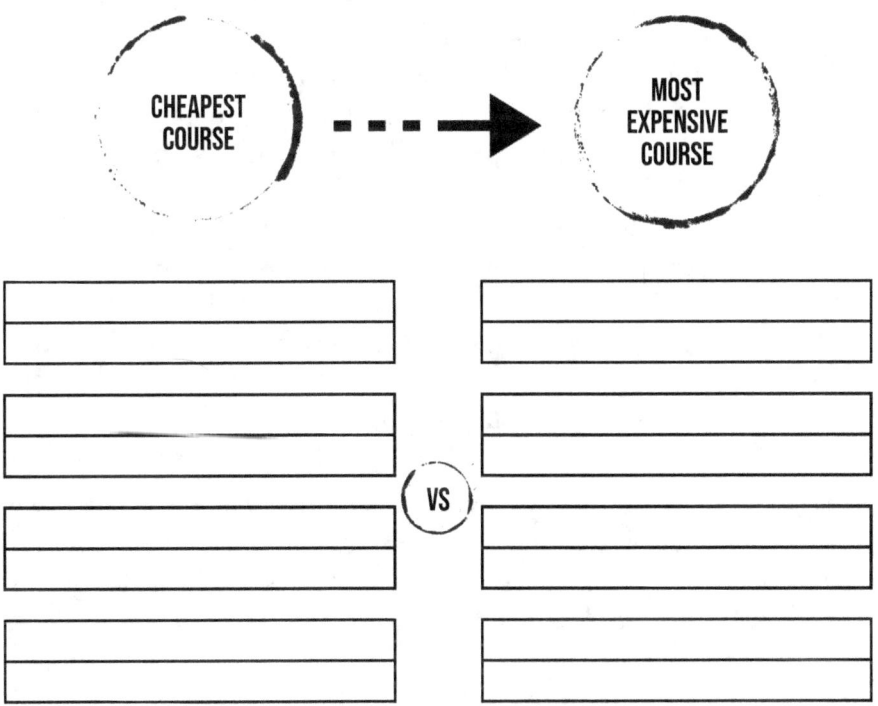

What Is The Rule Of 40?

Used by software companies, the "Rule of 40" is used to assess the health of a business by calculating the sum of its growth rate % and profit margin. **If it's greater than 40, the business is in good shape.**

What Would You Do?

After creating the Blockchain 101 course we discussed earlier, my client decided to charge $499 for it. He was able to justify this price tag because of his expertise. Furthermore, he already had an extensive network of students on LinkedIn he knew he could market the course to. **As expected, demand was strong.**

The course sold well at $499 and even better when my client offered discounts and coupons, bringing the price down to $399.

It was apparent to both of us that $399 was *"the right price."*

What now?

Imagine it's 2026, and we revisit the Blockchain 101 course we created in 2022. We studied the analytics and sales data and found that while it's still getting some sales, the course is no longer as popular as it used to be. *What do we do now?*

Answer: It really depends on the problem.

Possible Outcomes

1. People may have lost interest in blockchain technology and moved on to the latest new thing. If that's the case, then there really isn't much you can do except create another course about a more in-demand topic.
2. The issue might also be that the information in the course has now become outdated compared to what's in newer courses. In that case, the right thing to do would be to release an updated version of the same course that includes up-to-date materials and resources for your students.
3. Falling sales could also reflect that the price we're charging is too high now. After all, no one knows what the market for courses about blockchain technology will look like in 2026… if there isn't a lot of supply right now, that might change in the future. Update your price accordingly.

My advice to you is that you should constantly be revising the prices of all the courses you make in response to market conditions.

This is called dynamic pricing.

Airlines use it. You should use it too.

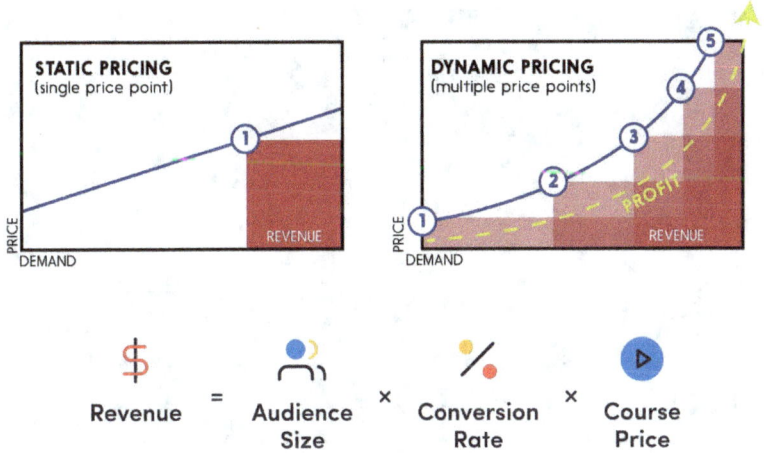

HOW MUCH DO ONLINE COURSES COST TO CREATE?

$177 (ON AVERAGE)

BUT CAN RANGE

$144 ----> $10,800

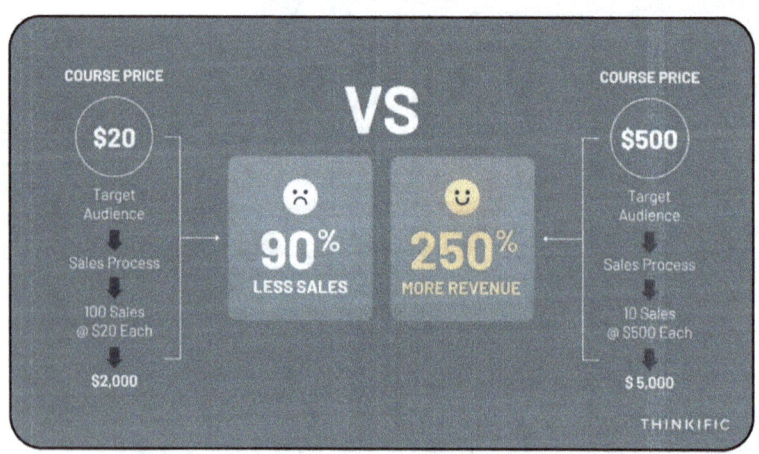

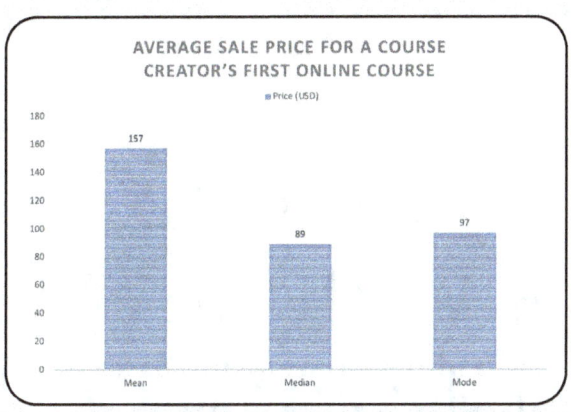

...according to a sample of 12,818 course creators

HOW MUCH DO FIRST TIME COURSE CREATORS SELL THEIR COURSES FOR?

$157
(ON AVERAGE)

PART III

CHAPTER SEVEN

"HOW TO PROMOTE YOUR COURSE ORGANICALLY"

"Many companies have forgotten they sell to actual people. Humans care about the entire experience, not just the marketing or sales or service."
– Dharmesh Shah

THINKING OUTSIDE THE BOX

Promoting your online course and securing your first sale may seem daunting. Please believe me when I say you have my full sympathies. However, you should also know that there are plenty of different methods you can use to get your first online sale.

Don't let marketing your course stress you out!

It's a walk in the park, if you know what you're doing.

Many first-time course creators will use paid advertising on Google, YouTube, Facebook, Instagram, TikTok, and LinkedIn to drive traffic and interest to their websites and online courses.

Some new and innovative course marketplaces, like Forento, even enable course creators to run these advertising campaigns natively through the Forento dashboard.

While paid advertising is something you should definitely consider, in this chapter we will focus on some of the free things you can do to promote your online course. Join my mailing list here for resources on paid advertising and best practices for SEO and ad targeting.

Things You Should Know

- 38% of all first-time course creators make their first sale in the first two weeks after the launch of their online course
- 58% will have made their first sale by the 4-week mark
- 69% will have made their first sale by the 6-week mark
- 76% will have made their first sale by the 8-week mark
- The remaining 23% make their first sale >3 months

TREAT YOUR ONLINE COURSE AS A PRODUCT LAUNCH

I recommend you put up your course for sale sometime before its release date. If you do that, you'll have much more valuable time to engage with your clients and promote interest in your course product. **Your online course is a product you are trying to sell.**

Treat it like one!

This means you should set up a website for your course with a landing page that's professional, clean, and (most importantly) user friendly. Please set up your own personal website, even if you plan to sell your course on a course marketplace like Udemy.

On your course website landing page, you must make the following absolutely clear to anyone visiting your website:

- *What is your course about?*
- *Who is your course for?*
- *What will those who take the course be able to do?*
- *Why are you qualified to teach this material?*

You're essentially turning the two-line mission statement you came up with in Chapter Three into a clear and convincing sales pitch.

> ### *Top Tip Time*
>
> Keep the sales pitch brief! Absolutely no one wants to read thousands of words of marketing and self-promotion.
>
> Your landing page should contain all that I mentioned in the bullet point above and should be no more than 200 words long. Stick to the word count. Period.

Exercise #9

Write down the details of what you plan to include on your website's landing page.

What is your course about?

Who is your course for?

What will those who take the course be able to do?

Why are you qualified to teach this material?

After you make your sales pitch, consider adding a section with a number of, **"Self Qualifying Questions."** These are questions that your clients can ask themselves before signing up for your course to evaluate whether or not this course is right for them.

The reason why this sales strategy works so well is because... it's interactive! It engages your audience. The questions should be deep and personal, allowing your potential clients to reflect on their deepest desires, priorities, and motivations in life.

Naturally, this creates an emotional response in the brain, which makes your sales pitch more memorable. Trust me, I'm a doctor.

Here's a template for Self Qualifying Questions:

This Course Is The Course For You IF

1. You're looking for a true and tried system you can follow to do/accomplish [INSERT COURSE OUTCOME]
2. What you need is someone to look up to and a community of like-minded people to share ideas and collaborate with
3. You're willing to do the work, watch all pre-recorded videos, and attend the live Q&A sessions and workshops
4. You understand that there are no shortcuts to success but that following any system is better than no system at all
5. You're committed to changing your life by putting in the work and are ready to explore new possibilities

Alternatively, you can consider being a little more mean:

This Course Is NOT The Course For You IF

1. You're **NOT** willing to do the work, watch all the content, and attend the live Q&A sessions and workshops
2. You **DON'T** believe in the value of lifelong learning
3. You're looking for a shortcut to success because you believe you **DON'T** need to work hard to succeed
4. You **DON'T** believe in the value of collaborative work and **DON'T** think you have anything to learn from others
5. You're **NOT** committed to changing your life by putting in the work and are **NOT** ready to explore new possibilities

MAKE USE OF CALL-TO-ACTION BUTTONS

Make sure to include a button on your landing page that takes users to a page where they can learn more about your course.

This page should provide your website visitors with a detailed breakdown of the various modules, lessons, teaching methods, and learning outcomes. It's on this page that, once you've captured your customer's interest, you make it abundantly clear to them that your online course is also technically rigorous.

Once they're done reading, include another link redirecting customers to where they can purchase your course. This can be through your website or your chosen marketplace.

Something that you must include as part of your website is a pop-up message asking website visitors to sign up for your mailing list.

Why?

Because, ultimately, most people who visit your website will not buy your course, so you must collect their contact details (email).

Once you have their emails, these people will be a part of your wider community and audience, despite not having made a purchase! You'll be able to keep in touch with them and work on building your relationship with them with your weekly emails. If you do this, you'll build a repertoire with them over time, and they will be significantly more likely to buy your course in the future.

To incentivise website visitors to sign up for your mailing list, you should offer them exclusive bonus content in exchange for their emails. This can include a short introductory webinar, an e-book, or access to your private Discord server or Reddit community.

You can also promise them discount codes and other perks, though I find that offering free introductory webinars and e-books often works best. The trick is to send these perks directly to their inboxes so they're left with no choice but to give you their real email addresses.

Top Tip Time

Most course creators find that they must initially sell their online courses through a trusted marketplace.

However, as your business grows, you should expect to move away from relying on third-party marketplaces and, instead, sell your online course through your website.

This should absolutely be your end goal.

Eliminate the middle man and self-host. Profit.

You will never be able to do this, however, unless you begin building a community around your brand. Get those emails.

CRAFT YOUR SALES PITCH AROUND YOUR CUSTOMER'S NEEDS

When promoting their course on their website, online marketplaces, and social media, too many course creators will focus entirely on how packed with information their online course is. This will include mentioning the number of hours of video, audio, and all the other resources the course contains.

While it's generally a good idea to highlight to prospective buyers that your course is good value for money, you must never forget that your audience is driven, first and foremost, by results. Customers are far more likely to respond to your sales pitch if you tell them what they will be able to do — once they complete your course.

You should, therefore, include this section on your landing page:

"By The End Of This Course You Will"

- Write these down in bullet point list format
- Be specific and avoid technical jargon at all costs
- Use the intended learning outcomes (ILOs) discussed in Chapter Four for inspiration on what to write

It's difficult, however, to create a sales pitch that is centred around your customers' needs if you don't know your customers well.

The Golden Rule

"Know Your Customer"

The better you know your customers, the easier it will be to sell your courses to them.

To demonstrate your expertise and generate traction for your course, host free 30-60 minute long webinars and other live events where your followers can ask you questions directly.

Schedule one free live event each week for the eight to twelve weeks leading up to the launch of your online course.

These live events can take more or less any format you like, and variety is great!

Start with a pre-scheduled live webinar on your website, YouTube or Twitch. These webinars offer a great opportunity for your audience to interact with you directly and ask questions.

You can also even use Reddit and Twitter.

Both platforms are currently experimenting with rooms where users can converse à la Clubhouse *(lol, remember that?)*. You can even host your own AskMeAnything in a relevant Reddit community. These live events are invaluable in giving you the exposure you need to showcase your expertise and credibility to your audience.

The likelihood of potential clients making a purchase increases exponentially with each live session or webinar they attend.

Keep hosting these webinars and follow a regular schedule.

At the end of each webinar, do everything you can to collect as many email addresses, as these emails will be what you use to inform your audience of your next webinar. **Build that relationship.**

Exercise #10

Use the template below to create a weekly content calendar for your social media accounts and live webinars. The key is consistency, so stick to it!

MONDAY
☐
☐
_____
_____
_____

TUESDAY
☐
☐
_____
_____
_____

WEDNESDAY
☐
☐
_____
_____
_____

THURSDAY
☐
☐
_____
_____
_____

FRIDAY
☐
☐
_____
_____
_____

SATURDAY

SUNDAY

Exercise #11
Once you've hosted your first webinar, go back to your audience a few days later and ask them for their feedback using the sample questionnaire below.

---

1. WHAT DID YOU THINK OF ME & THE QUALITY OF TEACHING IN THE WEBINAR?

2. WHAT WERE YOUR FAVOURITE PARTS OF THE WEBINAR?

3. IS THERE ANYTHING ELSE YOU WISH I'D COVERED IN THE WEBINAR?

You must refer your audience to your online course at the end of each webinar they attend. The way to do this is to say that while you're more than happy to continue answering questions and teaching people about this topic, you actually have a comprehensive course that contains everything they need to know.

Describe the additional things the viewer will learn if they take your paid course, and emphasise the support and accountability you provide all your students.

No reasonable person will judge you for keeping some of your content behind a paywall, especially if they're already learning so much from you for free! In fact, they'll be grateful.

> Don't be self-conscious about marketing yourself and your work. There is absolutely nothing wrong with hustling, so long as you know how it's done.

GATHER TESTIMONIALS BEFORE YOU LAUNCH

Another excellent way to show your clients that you're well-placed to be their teacher is to provide them with testimonials from your former students.

You should secure these testimonials as early as possible.

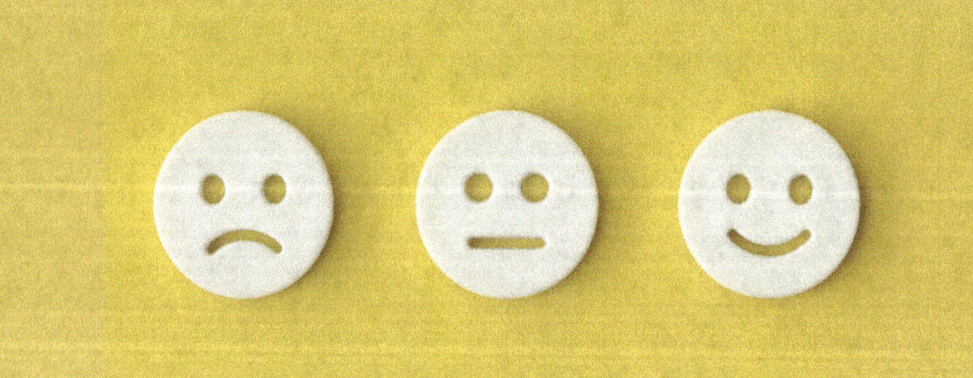

Here's Why

- They present you as an expert in your niche
- They humanise you and make you trustworthy
- Testimonials are an excellent way of illustrating the degree of support and accountability you offer in your course

However, you may wonder how you're meant to go about getting your first testimonial if you haven't even made your first sale (yet).

Here's How

1. If you've done everything we've described in this book so far, you should already have a small (but growing) group interested in you and the topic you plan to teach
2. Reach out to your online community and offer them early access to your course as part of your *"beta test group"*
3. Provide them with a promo code that either gives your course away for free or at a heavy discount
4. Once they've completed the course, request that they write you a review that you can include on your website, chosen course marketplace, and advertising material

What Is The "Beta Test Group?"

Your beta test group are the members of your community who are the first to see the finished product. They give you the testimonials you need but also provide you with feedback so you can make some minor adjustments to your course, fine-tune your teaching style, and make any final modifications to your teaching materials and resources.

The testimonials you receive from your "Beta Test Group" will often be what push potential buyers across the finish line and make them complete their purchases.

If you're making an online course for the first time, you must have a beta test group. This group needs to only be four to ten people strong. Please do this.

Do it for me. Do it for you. Just do it.

Read This Next

Questionnaire Design is a complete handbook for the mounting challenge of acquiring more data in less time, generating an entire rethink on how data is collected.

Looking At The Broader Picture

Many course creators don't like the idea of offering their entire online course for free and will often discourage others from doing it. This is understandable because, after all, no one likes giving out months of their hard work away for nothing — *or charging people significantly less for it than what it's worth!*

However, you're actually getting something very valuable in return. **Feedback. Testimonials. Reviews.**

Individually, these can be worth far more than the $100 you get from selling the course to that one customer.

A single testimonial, or positive review, will often translate to many future clients and significantly more long-term revenue.

If you're still unconvinced, remember that you should think in terms of what's best for your online course business rather than what's best for your course. **Look at the broader picture.**

When I first started writing online course video scripts, it took me over a year before I got my first client. Once I had their five-star review, I got my next client the very next month.

CREATE A FREE 1 HOUR MINI-COURSE FOR YOUTUBE

Like it or not, YouTube has become the first place people will go when they want to learn something new.

There are more than 2.6 billion active users on YouTube, and frankly, the exposure that the world's biggest video-sharing platform provides is utterly priceless. Most people know that Google is the most visited website in the world. What a lot of people don't know is that YouTube is the second most visited.

I recommend that every serious course creator of any kind have some presence on YouTube. Once you have a presence on YouTube, you'll be able to leverage this exposure to showcase your expertise and promote your online course and other e-learning products.

Approach #1	*Approach #2*
You can create videos exclusively for YouTube and grow an organic follower base on the platform, which you can later use to promote your course and any other products you create.	Once you're done creating your course, repurpose some of your videos that can work as standalone content to create a shorter free version of a single module for YouTube.

I don't recommend you go for Approach #1.

YouTube is a lot of work. YouTube is hard labour.

The competition is fierce.

There are professional YouTubers out there who spend 80+ hours each week creating YouTube videos. You'll burn yourself out if you create exclusive content for YouTube on top of creating your online courses and managing your business. You have an online course to make and promote. **You're not a YouTuber!**

You're merely leveraging the power of YouTube to promote your business. Focus on that. Don't allow yourself to get distracted.

Instead, opt for Approach #2.

Repurpose a module that you know would interest a large portion of your audience and covers some core principles and create a free mini-course version of it for YouTube. The YouTube mini course is an ad for your full course, meaning that people will judge

5 KEY YOUTUBE STATISTICS

YouTube has

$2.6 BILLION

users worldwide.

62%
of global consumers use YouTube.
(Statista, 2021)

Everyday people watch

1 BILLION

hours of video on YouTube generate billions of views.

(YouTube, 2019)

62%
of businesses use YouTube as a channel to post video content.
(Buffer, 2019)

90%
of people say they discover new brands or products on YouTube.
(Think with Google, 2019)

the quality of the full paid version based on the free mini course they watch on YouTube. Don't cut any corners with the free version.

Your YouTube mini-course must be just as good as your paid online course.

Once you've decided what content to put out on YouTube, upload the videos in the form of self-contained five to ten minute lessons. **This works best when you're teaching your audience quick fixes, tips, or tricks in 5-10 minute videos.**

For example, suppose you're creating a video editing course. Consider making a series of five minute videos teaching the basics of video editing. Choose the videos to be about topics that a lot of inexperienced video editors commonly struggle with, like using a greenscreen, sound editing, or video colour grading.

Once you have several videos out, create a playlist that features all your individual videos. The YouTube algorithm will love you.

The Best Part?

Many of your viewers will likely watch these 5-minute video guides from start to finish. YouTube's algorithm will, therefore, be incentivised to recommend your videos to a broader audience and will do all the hard work of finding your target audience for you.

Having experienced your teaching style and the quality of your content, these YouTube viewers will feel persuaded to buy your course. This only works, however, if you directly reference the full paid version of your course in each and every single video you upload

Read This Next

Hook Point breaks down the most effective strategies to generate new opportunities, innovate and scale your business, and create a compelling brand.

onto YouTube.

This "Call-To-Action" (CTA) should only be made after you have provided the viewer with value, so the viewer perceives you as an expert, first and foremost, rather than a "hack" with a product they're trying to sell.

Value first, and then your sales pitch.

However, this doesn't mean that you place your sales pitch right at the very end of your YouTube video. This isn't ideal as, by the end of your video, most of your audience will either have stopped watching or be preparing to. Instead, you should place your call-to-action after you've provided value, but before 50% of your video.

Top Tip Time

Don't forget to include a link to your website landing page underneath each video you publish on YouTube and in your channel description. Beyond being an effective sales strategy, adding links to your website in as many places on the internet will improve the rankings of your website on search engines.

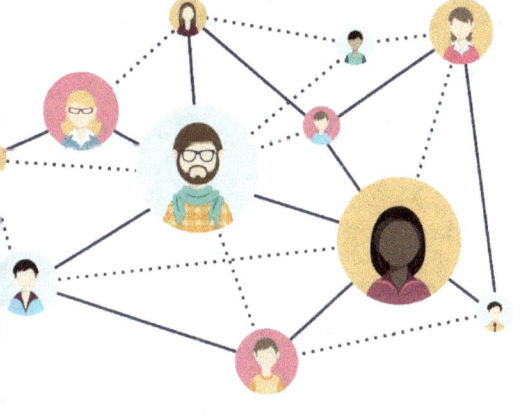

Don't Allow Yourself To Get Distracted!

Many online course creators frequently get lost in the YouTube ecosystem and lose sight of what YouTube means to them.

As an online course creator, you must never forget that Google AdSense isn't what your business revenue model relies on.

It's not your primary source of income.

You should, therefore, not spend your valuable time chasing views and subscribers. *Why?* Because you're only interested in using YouTube to target and reach a select group of people interested in your topic/niche.

To do this, you don't need hundreds of thousands of subscribers.

You're better off with a smaller (yet, more loyal) following on YouTube that consists of ten thousand subscribers or so.

If in the future, you find your YouTube channel gaining a fair bit of traction, and your subscriber base begins to grow significantly, you may consider pivoting your business model towards YouTube and away from online course creation.

That's a discussion for another book I'll write at some point in the future, however.

Read This Next

The YouTube Formula provides the secrets to getting the results that every YouTube creator and strategist wants and explores the YouTube algorithm.

THE WEBINAR FUNNEL

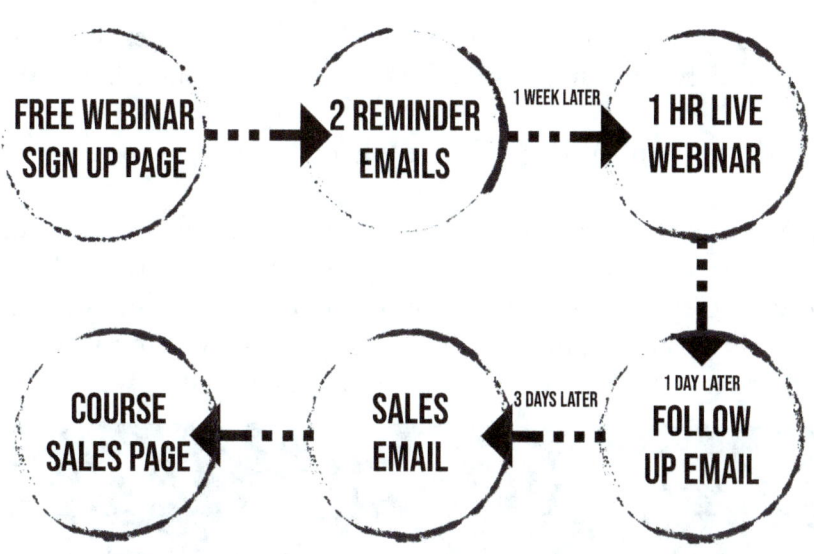

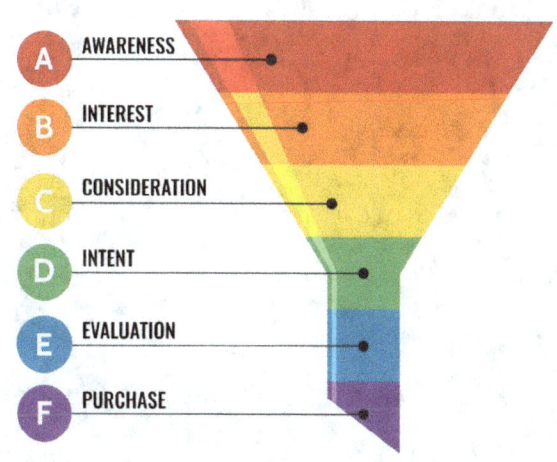

NETWORKING TO SCALE & EXPAND YOUR BUSINESS

After making your first few sales, you will want to scale up your business, driving even more traffic to your course and website.

The best way to do this is by becoming a respected expert in your niche, which you can do through collaborations with other creators.

Look for experts in your field and engage with them.

Leverage your growing following and new-found credibility to approach these experts with partnership proposals. As with everything else, these partnerships must be mutual. They must have something you want that they can offer you, and you must be able to offer them something else in return that they need or want.

As you only have a small audience right now, you may think that the only thing you have to offer is monetary compensation. **It's not.**

You can also offer:

- To promote their work to your audience
- The rights to use bits and pieces of your content
- The credibility of being associated with you

If you're still unconvinced, consider what the world's most popular podcast host, Joe Rogan, has to gain from inviting speakers onto his show. The people Rogan invites to his podcast show don't pay him monetarily for the exposure they receive by appearing on the world's most popular podcast show.

However, they do pay him with their credibility and content.

Most course creators I've had the pleasure of working with wrongly believe that they are *"too small"* to approach and collaborate with more prominent creators. Please stop. Stop that mindset.

There is no such thing as too small.

1. Create a list of podcasters and YouTubers in your niche.
2. On that list, write down the type of content that they create and the size of each creator's audience.
3. Request an invitation to speak to their audiences about your area of expertise. Make your expectations and what you're willing to offer absolutely clear to them. Don't forget to leverage your testimonials and course as evidence of your credibility, knowledge, and expertise.
4. Prepare to be surprised at how many of these content creators will get back to you and will be happy to feature you or promote your work – in exchange for the content, interest, and credibility they can get from you.

PART IV

CHAPTER EIGHT
"GROW YOUR AUDIENCE & ONLINE COMMUNITY"

"Never treat your audience as customers, always as partners." – James Stewart

Once you've sold your online course to your first few customers, your priority should now be to grow your audience and online following. **This is how you scale up.**

The larger your online following, the higher your revenue will be.

As old-fashioned as it may seem, email is still the best way to connect with and grow your audience. Yes. You heard that right. Email.

It's 2022, and I'm telling you, a mailing list trumps a following on the best social media platforms out there. *But why is that exactly?*

Many online course creators will choose to ignore email completely and will not create a robust email offering for their subscribers. Instead, they'll go down the route of building their online following on social media platforms like Facebook, Instagram, Twitter, YouTube, or LinkedIn. That's fine. It's better than fine.

These platforms give you access to a massive pool of potential customers that you can tap into. This makes social media apps invaluable as you can use them to promote and sell your content and course, and promote your online business and brand.

It's essential, however, that you remember you do not control your relationship with and access to your fans and audience when you use these social media platforms.

The apps are the ones that control and gate-keep that relationship.

For example, you may have 100,000 people who follow you on Facebook, but should Facebook decide to restrict or altogether ban your account, you risk losing your access to your audience.

You might think that would never happen to you. Fair.

However, remember that Facebook (and all the other platforms) are constantly tweaking their content policies and algorithms.

If one day, you find yourself on the wrong side of an algorithm update, you may find your access to your audience significantly diminished. You'll notice your reach and engagement metrics plummet as the algorithm shows your posts and content to fewer and fewer people.

It doesn't matter how great your posts are in situations like this.

The algorithm still won't show it because your content no longer aligns with the objectives of the platform you're using.

Example: How The TikTok Algorithm Works

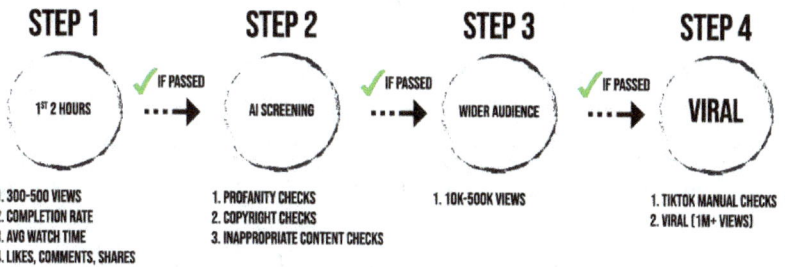

Example: How The Facebook Algorithm Works

Content Quality Scoring	Does it include a native image or video? Yes / No Does it include external links? Yes / No Is it clickbait? Yes / No Does post ask to like, comment, or share? Yes / No Does it include words like "free" "sale" or "promotion?" Yes / No Has the same post been used before? Yes / No	
Shows Post To 1% Of Fans To Measure Engagement	*Algorithmic Signals*	Like = +1pt Comment = +6pt Share = +13pt 3 second Video View = +4pt 60 second Video View = +13pt Hide Post / Report Page = -100pt
Ranking Signals	Is it timely and does it reference a trending topic? Yes / No Is the page regularly producing high quality content and live videos? Yes / No Are people who regularly engage with your page engaging? Yes / No Is your community having back and forth discussions in the comments? Yes / No Are the post types what people engage with regularly? Yes / No	

In other words, social media apps will only promote your work organically so long as you, your business, and your content's objectives align with their objectives.

For example, Facebook's algorithm has changed over the past few years to hide posts from businesses that:
- promote a product or an app
- offer promotions, discounts, or coupons
- reuse ad content exactly without any changes
- directs people to an external website

These changes have seen some businesses' organic reach on Facebook fall to less than one percent.

I think the message is clear.

Don't let Facebook, or any other social media platform, control your relationship with your audience. Your fans. Your content.

Your business. You should be in control.

I wouldn't put my livelihood in the hands of an algorithm because, as I've illustrated above, **algorithms are fickle.** That's precisely why your electronic mailing list must be your top priority.

By all means, establish a presence on Facebook, Instagram, LinkedIn or TikTok— but make your mailing list the priority.

Most employed adults check their emails every morning. It's been this way since the 90s. Facebook has been around for barely a decade, and people have already started logging in less and less. I'm not saying Facebook is a sinking ship. I haven't (*yet*) decided if it is, but what I know for sure is that Facebook has proved itself to be far more ephemeral than email. You need to collect those emails.

While this may *seem* difficult, it really isn't.

Here's how to go about it:
1. Go through the course you've just created
2. Select a couple of popular topics from your course and condense the material into a single video tutorial or PDF
3. Upload the file(s) to your website, locking it behind a "subscribe with email to download" pop up message
4. Promote the file(s) on social media as a free guide for anyone who's interested in your topic/niche
5. Sit back and watch the email addresses come in

Not everyone will agree with me here, but I think email addresses are personal information. And as you're asking for personal information, you should avoid "spooking" your subscribers by asking for too many bits and pieces of information. All you need is a list of email addresses to create an electronic mailing list.

You should, therefore, only ask for an email address for maximum conversion. Nothing more. Nothing less. Don't get clever and start asking for residential addresses and telephone numbers.

> *Top Tip Time*
>
> To avoid people signing up with fake email addresses, consider emailing the PDF file or a link to the video tutorial directly to the email address they give you when signing up.

YOUR EMAIL NEWSLETTER MUST DELIVER VALUE

It's no secret that most of us receive way too many emails on a daily basis. Most of these emails end up deleted before they're even opened. **They're essentially spam.** However, every single one of us has two or three newsletters that we open and read religiously.

We practically never skip an email from these newsletters.

We may even *pay a membership fee to* receive those emails.

They tend to be newsletters that we "count on" because they give us valuable information that keeps us looped in and up-to-date.

Now, please take a moment to sit back and think about your favourite email newsletters and why you're subscribed to them.

What makes them so important to you?

Is it because they provide cutting-edge intel that makes you better at your job? Do they offer vital investment advice?

Perhaps they deliver daily bursts of motivation and tips that inspire you to create content and grow your business?

Or, maybe they just entertain you with a running list of the latest celebrity drama? The juicy celebrity gossip you talk about to your friends and family when you see them.

The newsletters I just mentioned are all very different from each other. And yet, they all achieve the same result.

They're able to attract readers and keep them engaged week after week with their interesting content. **They're not considered spam.**

To not be considered spam, your email newsletter should also be interesting. Don't just use your newsletter to promote your online course or recycle its content. Use the newsletter as an opportunity to deliver something extra. Something interesting.

Your newsletter should have something valuable.
It should be something your readers can grow to need.

6 STEPS TO EMAIL MARKETING SUCCESS

1
REVIEW OTHER SUCCESSFUL EMAIL NEWSLETTERS

2
DEFINE YOUR NEWSLETTER GOALS

3
SET THE READERS' EXPECTATIONS UPFRONT

4
CHOOSE THE BEST SERVICE PROVIDER

5
OFFER VALUE. PERIOD.

6
PUBLISH REGULARLY. BE. CONSISTENT.

You should create a newsletter with **a regular publishing schedule.**

I recommend you start with a once-a-week newsletter and publish it at the same time and day every week. Crucially, each newsletter should offer your subscribers something they can rely on. This can be intel, advice, inspiration, entertainment, or whatever.

Just make sure it works in harmony with your niche and adds to your business model rather than distracts from it. Cohesion.

Exercise #12

Use the space below to write down ideas for your weekly email newsletter. Remember that the key here is value and consistency! Feel free to check out other newsletters in your niche for inspiration. No one will judge you!

My recommendation if you're just starting out with your newsletter offering is to create a weekly newsletter and a monthly newsletter:
- Your weekly newsletter should offer audiences an actionable idea, along with some interesting insight.
- Your monthly newsletter should be a special edition where you publish interviews, case studies, in-depth analyses.

Combined, these two newsletters will incentivise loyalty and trust among your current fan base and, over time, will help grow your community.

START YOUR ONLINE COURSE BUSINESS TODAY

Exercise #13

Use the template below to plan your email newsletter offering. Include your goals and target audience, platform you will use, and how you plan to collect subscriptions.

WHAT IS YOUR GOAL WITH YOUR NEWSLETTER?

HOW WILL YOU COLLECT EMAILS?
-
-
-
-

WHICH PLATFORM WILL YOU USE?

HOW FREQUENT WILL YOUR EMAILS BE?

WHAT TIME/DAY WILL YOU SEND EMAILS?

WHAT CONTENT WILL YOUR EMAILS INCLUDE?
-
-
-
-

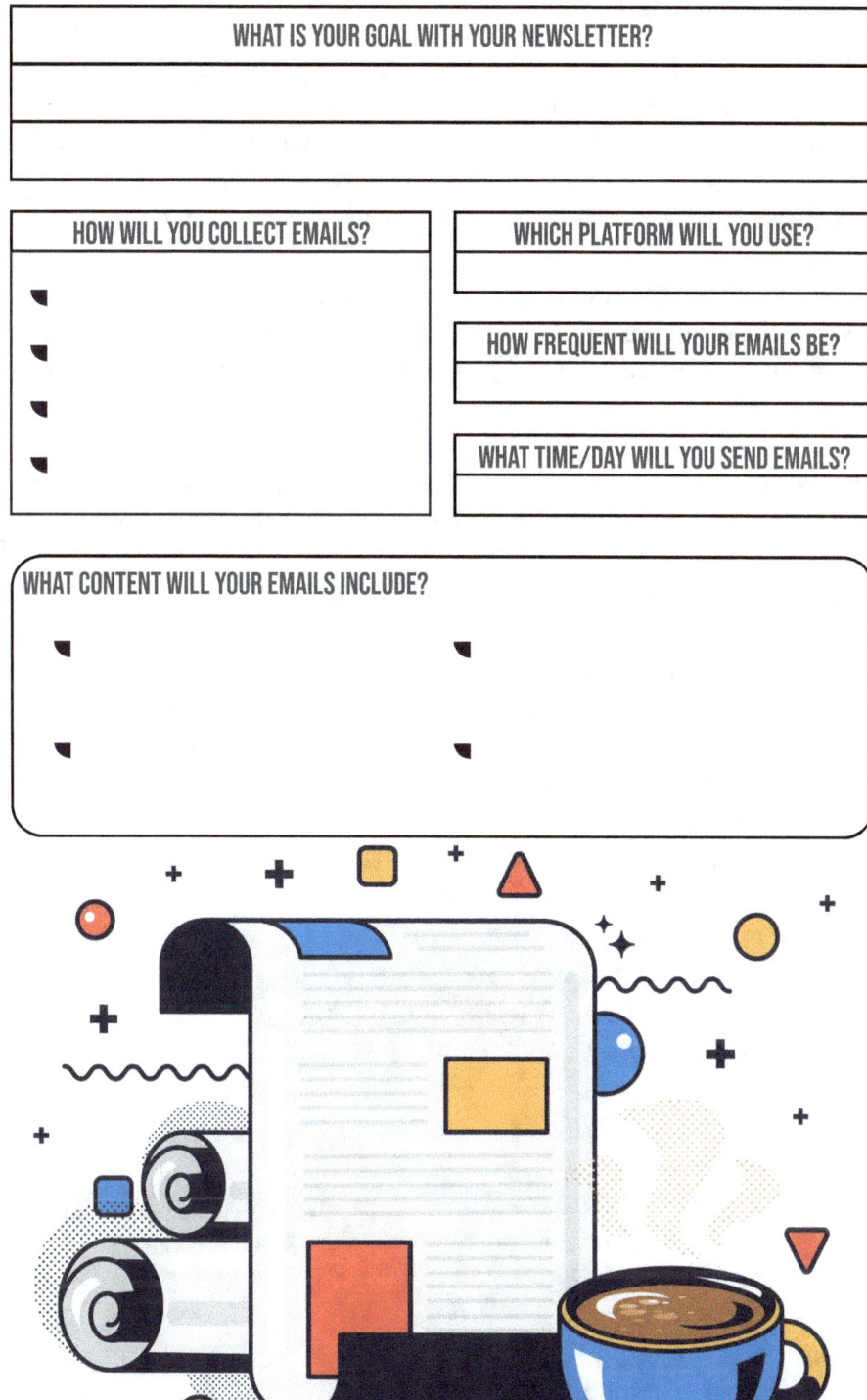

AUTORESPONDERS

Autoresponders are emails that are automatically generated based on subscriber behaviour. The most commonly used autoresponder is the "Welcome Email," which I'm sure you're familiar with. It welcomes a subscriber to a particular mailing list when they first subscribe. *Now, why should you care about them?*

These autoresponders are significantly more likely to be opened by readers. The autoresponder is probably this person's first interaction with your business and brand. It's their first impression of you. That's why you must craft these emails with great attention.

Instead of the typical and tired "Welcome Email," why don't you use that first email to create a personal relationship with the reader?

You can do this by using the following template:

1. Briefly greet the reader and thank them for subscribing.
2. Describe to them the kind of content your newsletter provides its readers. Include some recent examples.
3. Mention success stories and testimonials from your past students. What did the people who used your ideas and took your online course go on to achieve?
4. Ask the reader what issues they face and the kind of content they'd like to see from you in the future.
5. Remind them this isn't like any newsletter they've subscribed to in the past. Your newsletter is unique.
6. Thank them once again and sign off.

Read This Next

300 Email Marketing Tips gives you the framework you need in place to create a successful email marketing strategy for your business, through branding power.

It's important you remember that the "Welcome Email," doesn't have to be the only autoresponder you use.

One of my clients had an autoresponder set up that would go out at the end of every quarter to subscribers with the highest email open rates. My client rewarded these loyal readers with a 20 minute one-on-one Zoom call as a show of gratitude.

In those 20 minute they could ask her anything they wanted.

It's easy to see how this small gesture could turn loyal readers into superfans who go on to continue reading your newsletter and promote your work organically within their social circles.

What Are Autoresponders?

An autoresponder is a script that automates email replies. The script is triggered by user actions either on a site or when a user sends an email directly to another email with an autoresponder in place. Confirmation emails constitute the most common example of autoresponders, but autoresponders also have a variety of other uses.

PROMOTING ON SOCIAL MEDIA

Once you've settled on your email newsletter offering, you will want to choose one or two social media platforms to use to promote your course and business. However, before you go out and set up your social media accounts, remember what your goals are:

- drive up traffic to your website
- drive up sales of your course
- drive up subscriptions to your mailing list

You mustn't try to do too many things at once.

Don't try to establish a presence on too many platforms simultaneously. Not only will this distract and confuse you, but it will also greatly hinder your efforts and slow down your growth.

If you've tried sharing the same content on different social media platforms in the past, you may have noticed that posts that perform well on some platforms often perform poorly on others.

> Your posts need to be specifically tailored to the audience and algorithm of the platform you choose to use.
>
> This will be almost impossible for you to do if you decide to conquer all the social media apps at the same time.
>
> Focus.

Focus on only one or two platforms — at least initially.

Your choice of which platform to use will invariably depend on your niche. That said, I think YouTube and Reddit are the most obvious choice for most online course creators, though Quora works well for some educators too. YouTube is the number two search engine in the world (right after Google), and Reddit's Communities have much better engagement than Facebook Groups, primarily because Reddit doesn't penalise you like Facebook for using external links.

It should be relatively easy for you to turn bits and pieces of your course into long and short-form videos on YouTube. Include a CTA that directs your audience to your course, website, or mailing list. Don't forget to (very briefly) tell the viewer what they stand to gain from leaving YouTube, Facebook, or Reddit (or whatever platform they're on) and visiting your course landing page or website.

You can even go a step further.

If you want YouTube to organically promote your videos (and, therefore, your CTA), you will need to understand what YouTube's objectives are. In other words, what does YouTube care about?

Like any other company interested in profit, YouTube cares about its revenue, specifically its ad revenue. It wants to maximise ad revenue.

As these ads feature before, during, and after videos published on YouTube, YouTube will promote videos that are:

- engaging and keep viewers watching for as long as possible
- more than 8 minutes long to allow for a mid-roll ad
- advertiser-friendly in terms of their subject matter

To this end, YouTube promotes videos about popular or trending topics with a high click-through rate (CTR) and average view duration (AVD) and abide by its extensive content guideline policies.

Understanding how YouTube generates revenue makes the platform's goals and objectives clear to us, allowing us to align ourselves with those objectives. That's how you "hack into" a platform's algorithm.

This isn't easy, but if you manage to do this, you will significantly cut your marketing costs as social media apps will organically promote your content, course, and business. This approach is a significantly more concentrated (and better) effort than spreading yourself "too thin" by creating posts and sharing them on all platforms.

Exercise #14

Use the template below to write down what you will do to achieve your goals.

SOCIAL MEDIA PLATFORM #1

---

1. HOW WILL YOU USE THE PLATFORM TO DRIVE TRAFFIC TO YOUR WEBSITE?

-
-

2. HOW WILL YOU USE THE PLATFORM TO DRIVE SALES OF YOUR COURSE?

-
-

3. HOW WILL YOU USE THE PLATFORM TO DRIVE SUBSCRIPTIONS TO YOUR MAILING LIST?

-
-

SOCIAL MEDIA PLATFORM #2

---

1. HOW WILL YOU USE THE PLATFORM TO DRIVE TRAFFIC TO YOUR WEBSITE?

-
-

2. HOW WILL YOU USE THE PLATFORM TO DRIVE SALES OF YOUR COURSE?

-
-

3. HOW WILL YOU USE THE PLATFORM TO DRIVE SUBSCRIPTIONS TO YOUR MAILING LIST?

-
-

PART IV

CHAPTER NINE

"DIVERSIFY YOUR REVENUE MODEL & PASSIVE INCOME STREAMS"

"We spent zero dollars on advertising. We just had a YouTube video and that was it. We did a quarter million dollars in revenue, just in three weeks."
– Mark Rober

According to research, most people make money in only one or two ways. As a content creator, you have the unique opportunity to build a balanced and diversified revenue model. This is what sets successful content creator entrepreneurs, like you, apart from the rest of the competition:

1. They're able to build a scalable and high quality content-first business with a unique and dynamic brand...
2. ...they can leverage this business and their wide audience base to explore multiple avenues for monetisation...
3. ...which allows them to generate passive income and achieve financial freedom as discussed in Chapter One.

The first and most obvious revenue stream is selling your first online course. Ideally, you will want these sales to last well into the future. You can do this by regularly featuring old online courses you've created on your website and recommending your previous courses to anyone interested in buying your current course.

If you can, market your previous course as a foundational course that's tailored to the interested customer's needs.

Mention how your previous course is cheaper and a great way of learning about a particular topic for the first time. If done right, your sales pitch will capture qualified customers for your second and third online courses – while also redirecting interested customers browsing your new course to your older course offerings!

An alternative model you can utilise once you've created several courses in the same niche is to create an academy program.

As part of your academy program, your audience will pay a flat monthly/annual subscription fee to access all your online courses, past, current, and future.

An academy program only works, however, if all your courses belong to the same niche. You will also likely need to add exclusive perks like weekly live Q&A sessions or workshops that users can RSVP to in advance. Depending on the size of your academy program, you may be able to introduce membership tiers.

REUSE YOUR COURSE MATERIAL TO CREATE STANDALONE PRODUCTS

Another viable option for course creators is to identify the pieces of content they've created for their course that work as standalone products. For example, these can be the workbooks you've created for your course, which you then sell directly through Amazon's Kindle Direct Publishing (KDP) program or perhaps use one of Amazon's smaller competitors.

Depending on your niche and the quality of your workbook, this can be a very lucrative revenue stream. Similarly, you can expect to be paid ad revenue by Google if you upload enough videos to YouTube to reach the YouTube Partner Program's thresholds of 1,000 subscribers and 4,000 hours of public watch time.

Furthermore, you may wish to explore affiliate marketing by including affiliate links to products and services that you mention in your courses, books, website, or YouTube videos.

While the revenue streams mentioned above may be insignificant sums of money initially, they will grow as your business and brand recognition expands. The best part is that they're completely passive and don't involve any extra work on your end once they're set up.

They're just there doing their thing while you focus on creating more content and growing your brand.

PAID NEWSLETTER SUBSCRIPTIONS

Many journalists and bloggers have moved over to Substack and Medium and now collect revenue from subscriptions to their email newsletter articles. This is a potentially interesting revenue stream, as you don't need that many paying subscribers to earn a reasonable income from your paid newsletter offering.

For Example

 x  = $5,000/month

1,000 subscribers $5/month

Substack only takes a 10% cut in return.

That said, I think you should be absolutely clear with yourself about what you hope to achieve with your newsletter.

Do you intend for it to be a revenue stream, or will it be a tool to grow your online community and audience?

It will be hard for your newsletter to be both.

As a compromise, you can **set up two newsletters** (one free, one paid), with each newsletter performing its role in your business model. Substack allows you to start paid newsletters alongside free newsletters. I, myself, use Substack and highly recommend it.

ADVERTISING & SPONSORSHIP

While advertising and sponsorship can be a great source of additional revenue, you should avoid including messages from sponsors and advertisers in your online course.

You can probably get away with using Amazon affiliate links, as these links don't intrude on the overall viewing experience.

However, your audience will, rightfully, object to seeing sponsored content in a course they've already paid for. **You need to think about what's best for the long-term health of your business when you decide whether or not to accept sponsorship deals.**

A sponsor can bring in a nice bit of cash right now, but it may cost you money in the long run. Now that I think of it, that's one more reason you need a free newsletter offering…

It gives you significantly more flexibility and advertising space to offer the sponsors and partners you work with. Your audience will readily accept sponsored content on your free newsletter as they will recognise that they're getting something of value (your content, your time, your ideas) at no real cost to them. Furthermore, if your business model and niche allow for it, you should consider paid public speaking engagements and on-site training workshops.

Besides being an excellent opportunity to connect with your audience and fan base, they can be a revenue stream and allow you to create more content for your burgeoning business empire — especially if you record these speaking engagements to post later.

MERCHANDISE

Finally, something I don't see enough creators do is merchandise. *Anymore, at least.* Unfortunately, merchandising has acquired a bit of a bad reputation and isn't considered a very profitable revenue stream for content creators.

I don't think the problem is merchandise per se, however.

I believe the reason most merchandise doesn't turn out particularly profitable has more to do with **the type of merchandise** we've seen and become accustomed to. So far, the merchandise we've seen has largely been limited to t-shirts, mugs, and coasters and the business, brand, influencer, or creator's name cheaply plastered on them.

As an educator, however, you have the unique opportunity to create educational merchandise. Think posters, fabrics, art supplies, diaries, and planners. Think of things that are somehow related to your niche and topic that your customers need in their lives and use.

If your customers are going to use your merch and actually need it, they're very likely going to buy it.

If in doubt, you can always go back to your mailing list and ask your community and audience for their feedback. Ask them what kind of educational merchandise they'd like to buy, how much they'd be willing to pay for it, and whether they think it's a good idea or not.

You must know that the ideas mentioned above are non-exhaustive, and there is *(literally)* an infinite number of ways that you can monetise your business model and create additional revenue streams!

The world is your oyster, so get swimming.

BIBLIOGRAPHY

Ultimate Course Formula – Iman Aghay

Follow the proven formula Iman provides in this book, or to his audiences both small and large and you will not only save valuable time, but you will remove the frustration and disappointment due to the lack of know-how.

Content Inc. – Joe Pulizzi

An ingenious approach to business based on having a singular focus on audience, and building a loyal audience directly, provide the best, most nuanced understanding of what products ultimately make the most sense to sell.

Everybody Writes – Ann Handley

Expert guidance and insight into the process and strategy of content creation, production and publishing, with actionable how-to advice designed to get results, with rules that you can apply across all your online assets.

Practical Marketing Strategy – Julia McCoy

A field guide for the smartest content marketers who know that strategy is the key to thriving in our world of new marketing through content. Designed especially for people who run a business and looking to learn marketing strategy.

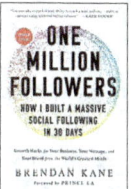

One Million Followers – Brendan Kane

The ultimate guide to building your worldwide brand and unlocking all the benefits social media has to offer, offering top tips for lead generation, e-commerce, direct response marketing, and revenue growth opportunities.

ABOUT THE AUTHOR

About The Author

Hesham Mashhour is a medical doctor and a University of Cambridge graduate.

Hesham has always been passionate about learning and education. In 2020, during the COVID pandemic, Hesham set up a YouTube channel that educates the public about the human brain, explaining how the brain works and how best to optimise its performance. From there, Hesham has worked with a range of online course creators and helped them launch their first online courses, providing them with support and guidance.

Some examples of online courses that Hesham has worked on include, "Overcoming The Toxic Mother Trauma," "Unpacking Your Anxiety & Finding Your Confidence," "Blockchain 101 For Computer Developers," "CV Writing For Educators In Higher Education," Forento's "How To Create An Online Course In 60 Days," and Nestle's "Employee Career Accelerator Program."

Most recently, Hesham led a 6 hour workshop on the topic of "Creating Interactive Digital Content For A-Level Students," and later this year, plans to launch his own online course where he will teach content creators about overcoming stress and preventing burnout. He is a keen cyclist and Taylor Swift fan.

You can contact him at hesham@betterbrainlab.com

https://www.betterbrainlab.com/

www.ingramcontent.com/pod-product-compliance
Lightning Source LLC
Chambersburg PA
CBHW071415210526
45465CB00001B/403